VGM Opportunities Seri

OPPORTUNITIES IN
METALWORKING
CAREERS

Mark Rowh

Revised Edition

Foreword by
Bruce Braker
President
Tooling & Manufacturing Association

VGM Career Horizons
NTC/Contemporary Publishing Group

Library of Congress Cataloging-in-Publication Data

Rowh, Mark.
   Opportunities in metalworking careers / Mark Rowh.—Rev. ed.
      p. cm. — (VGM opportunities series)
   ISBN 0-658-00200-7 (paperback) — ISBN 0-658-00198-1 (cloth)
    1. Metal-work—Vocational guidance. I. Title. II. Series.
TS213 .R694 2000
671'.023—dc21   99-53372
                                               CIP

Cover photograph: © PhotoDisc, Inc.

Published by VGM Career Horizons
A division of NTC/Contemporary Publishing Group, Inc.
4255 West Touhy Avenue, Lincolnwood (Chicago), Illinois 60712-1975 U.S.A.
Copyright © 2000 by NTC/Contemporary Publishing Group, Inc.
International Standard Book Number: 0-658-00198-1 (cloth)
                                          0-658-00200-7 (paper)

01 02 03 04 05 LB 15 14 13 12 11 10 9 8 7 6 5 4 3 2

DEDICATION

This book is dedicated to
Linda, Lisa, David, and Jenny Anne.

CONTENTS

About the Author . . . . **vii**

Foreword . . . .**viii**

Acknowledgments . . . . **xi**

Introduction . . . . **xii**

1. **Metalworking: An Overview** **1**

    How metalworking affects our lives. History of
    metalworking. Why pursue a metalworking career? Exploring
    further.

2. **Metalworking: A Diverse Technology** **11**

    The expansive nature of metalworking. Wide-ranging job
    possibilities.

3. **Sheet-Metal Working** **17**

    Job titles. Work performed. Working conditions. Skills
    needed to succeed. Learning the trade. Questions to ask
    yourself.

4. **Machining and Machine Operation** **28**

    Work of machinists. Work of machine operators. Job titles.
    Training options. Working environment.

5. Structural and Reinforcing Metalworking **39**

Jobs performed. Working environment. Skills needed for success. Training options.

6. Welding **47**

Welding processes. Job titles. Work performed. Job tasks. Skills and aptitudes needed. Developing welding skills.

7. Jewelry Making **59**

Work performed. Job titles. Special job features. Career advantages. Training options.

8. Getting Trained **67**

Apprenticeships. On-the-job training. Government-sponsored training programs. Programs offered by schools and colleges. Paying for training. Getting financial aid.

9. Earnings, Benefits, and Special Opportunities . . . **86**

Earnings. Benefits. Job openings. Expanding opportunities for women and minorities. Career possibilities for the handicapped.

10. Where to Go from Here **94**

Finding a job. Handling job interviews.

Appendix A: Further Reading. **97**

**Appendix B: Trade and Technical Schools
Offering Metalworking Programs** **98**

**Appendix C: Colleges Offering
Metalworking Programs** **108**

**Appendix D: Selected Organizations
Related to Metalworking.** **146**

ABOUT THE AUTHOR

Mark Rowh is Director of Institutional Advancement at New River Community College in Dublin, Virginia. His experience as an educator has included administrative positions at Greenville (South Carolina) Technical College, Bluefield (West Virginia) State College, and Parkersburg (West Virginia) Community College. In these positions, Rowh has worked closely with a variety of occupational programs. He holds a doctorate in vocational and technical education from Clemson University.

Rowh's articles on educational and management topics have appeared in more than fifty magazines. He has contributed several other books to the VGM Career Horizons series and is the author of *Coping with Stress in College,* published by College Board Books.

FOREWORD

The products of metalworking are everywhere. Computers are housed in plastic and metal containers formed by steel molds and fabricated by precision sheet-metal presses. The computers themselves contain metal parts stamped by metal dies. Manufacturers make computer workstation chairs and desks of metal or plastic or both. A woodworking machine made of metal crafts furniture made out of wood. If the chairs are upholstered, the fabric was woven on a loom made of metal.

The tooling and machining industry provides parts, machinery, and equipment for the manufacture of cars, household appliances, medical equipment, spacecraft and aircraft, business machines, electronics, agricultural implements, vehicles for transportation, and construction equipment. It is the basis for all of the manufacturing and construction industries, producing everything from stamping dies to steel molds for plastics, to die cast dies for molten metal, to machined component parts, to formed and cast metal parts, to the most sophisticated machine tools and automated production systems.

Precision metalworkers—machinists, tool and die makers, mold makers, and production machine tool set-up and operators—are highly skilled technologists and technicians who set up and operate machine tools and create finished parts or special tools. To accomplish this, they must read engineering drawings, know how much material is needed, and understand metal properties to use the best types of metals for the project. Metalworkers calculate machining processes such as cutting-tool speeds and feeds. They are skilled in manual machining and computer controlled machine tool programming, creating parts measured as closely as one thousandth or one ten-thousandth of an inch, or even as close as a micron (thirty-four millionths of an inch). Metalworkers must think creatively, blending analytical reasoning with imagination. Mold makers also must have an in-depth understanding of the qualities of plastic materials. Mold makers who make die cast dies must understand properties of such materials as zinc and aluminum.

These skilled men and women learn and perfect their craft in a combination of hands-on experience and training and classroom education—a demanding and rewarding process. Tooling or machining technologists can start with college-credit related theory hours, in addition to their hands-on experience, and progress all the way to associate, bachelor's, and graduate degrees in engineering technology or management. The opportunities for education, challenge, advancement, and financial success are excellent.

Thousands of metalworking companies across North America seek to hire people with the right attitudes, aptitudes, education, and skills. Candidates with strong math skills, communications skills, computer skills, mechanical aptitude, and a willingness to learn should pursue careers in precision metalworking. Best way to get started? Visit a local manufacturing plant and ask about careers in precision metalworking or contact an association of metalworking companies. Metalworking career opportunities abound for qualified people.

> Bruce Braker
> President
> Tooling & Manufacturing Association

ACKNOWLEDGMENTS

The author greatly appreciates the cooperation of the following organizations in the development of this book:

- Accrediting Commission of Career Schools and Colleges of Technology
- American Welding Society
- Career Training Foundation
- International Association of Machinists and Aerospace Workers
- National Tooling and Machining Association
- National Training Fund, Sheet Metal and Air Conditioning Industry
- New River Community College
- North American Die Casting Association
- RWM
- Tooling & Manufacturing Association

Some material also has been derived from the *Occupational Outlook Handbook,* 1998–99 edition, published by the U.S. Department of Labor.

INTRODUCTION

Choosing a career is one of life's most important decisions. Naturally, for any potential occupation, you should ask plenty of questions, including the following: What are the long-term expectations that workers will continue to be needed in the field? What kind of earning potential does the field offer? What approaches, skills, or special training will be needed to gain employment in the first place, as well as to succeed once hired? What tasks will be performed in carrying out the responsibilities of the job?

When it comes to a possible career in metalworking, the future holds significant promise. After all, metals are among the most basic materials used by human beings. People who build or repair metal goods or structures play an important role in our society. This has been true for many years and should continue into the future. Even though advances in technology have introduced new materials such as plastics and ceramics, metals will still be vital in the new century.

Given the continued importance of metal, jobs involved in working with it will continue to hold their own importance. The information provided here should prove helpful to anyone interested in pursuing a related career.

CHAPTER 1

METALWORKING: AN OVERVIEW

HOW METALWORKING AFFECTS OUR LIVES

Our civilization is based on a number of technological advancements. Unlike primitive men and women who used implements of stone and wood to shape their lives, modern people benefit from the use of a variety of materials from which tools, homes, factories, and other structures are built. And no single substance is more necessary than metal.

Just think about it. All around you, devices and structures made of metal play a key role in your life. Here are just a few examples:

- Cars, trucks, and buses are made in large part of steel, aluminum, and other metals.
- Houses, apartments, factories, and office buildings contain pipes, reinforcing rods, beams, and many other components made of metal.

- Various household appliances, from refrigerators to washers and dryers, are built from components that include metal.
- Airplanes, ships, trains, as well as other forms of transportation include large quantities of metal in their construction.
- Today's large bridges would be impossible to build without metal.
- Even the tools used to build the items described above are themselves made primarily of metal.

With the widespread use of metals as basic construction materials, the ability to work with them is a highly useful commodity. Persons who can cut, shape, fasten, or otherwise fashion metal parts into useful objects fill a variety of interesting positions.

Metalworking may consist of the construction of anything from jewelry to skyscrapers. It can be a simple process involving a few pieces of basic equipment or a highly technical effort making use of microprocessors and precise measurements. In some cases, the work performed will be the repair of existing items rather than the creation of new ones. Whatever the ultimate goal, metalworking requires special skills. This means that men and women who have developed these skills are needed by various types of employers. With the importance that different metals continue to have as building and repair materials, the work of trained metalworkers represents a promising career area.

HISTORY OF METALWORKING

Efforts to work with metal have a long and fascinating history. For thousands of years, the ability to create and use metal has been crucial to the development of human society. Historians have even used advances in such technology to label different eras, dubbing them the Bronze Age, Iron Age, and so forth.

Prehistoric Times

Long before modern civilization developed, the first human beings learned to use a variety of materials for tools, weapons, and other purposes. For example, prehistoric men and women chipped one stone against another to create a sharp edge for scraping hides or cutting apart animal carcasses. They developed the ability to make knives, arrowheads, spearheads, and other useful items in a similar fashion. Sometimes they used not only stone, but also other available substances, such as bone or wood. The first spear was probably nothing more than a sharpened stick, eventually enhanced by adding a point or head of a harder substance such as stone. What many generations of primitive people did not have, however, was metal.

No one in these prehistoric times knew how to extract metal from ores, nor how to melt it, shape it, or otherwise work with any type of it. Technology was limited to materials that were less durable, less malleable, or both. A piece of stone could be chipped and shaped to some extent, but the possibilities for using it were limited. The same was true of wood and other building materials.

Discovery of Metals

When human beings discovered metals and how to work with them, things changed dramatically. Probably the first to gain widespread use was copper, which is one of the softest and most easily worked metals. It seemed ideal for creating simple tools, cooking utensils, bracelets, necklaces, and other items. Other soft metals, such as gold and silver, also were found to be easily formed into objects such as jewelry or figurines for artistic or religious uses.

As time passed, these early people who worked with metal began to experiment with both materials and techniques. For example, they learned to combine two or more metals into a new material having different qualities than either of the original, separate metals. Combining copper with tin produced bronze, a metal that gained widespread use for purposes ranging from body armor to domestic utensils.

Once people began to use metal widely, they found it provided enormous advantages. Warriors equipped with metal shields and spears often held the upper hand in battle. Metal knives, axes, and other tools also proved highly effective for peaceful uses. All in all, the ability to work with various metals became an important element of every civilization.

Over thousands of years, the variety and quality of work with metal increased in many ways. Probably the most important advancement was the discovery of iron and steel. From ancient Roman times through the Middle Ages and on into the present, iron and steel have played an integral role in human technological development. In everything from agriculture to transportation, these strong and versatile metals have provided essential building materials.

Other metals such as aluminum and lead also have proven important as scientists, technicians, and workers in a wide range of fields have developed ways to manufacture and use them. Virtually every civilized society from ancient times to the present has made wide use of whatever metals were available at the time.

The Industrial Revolution

Many of the most significant developments in metalworking occurred during the Industrial Revolution of the 1700s and 1800s. During this time, the practice of mass production was initiated and expanded, and more and more metal objects were introduced into everyday life.

Some of the most important influences on the development of metalworking practices and techniques have included the following:

- the growth of railroads, which required hundreds of thousands of miles of tracks as well as metal components for the trains themselves
- advances in military technology, with increasingly sophisticated weapons and weapons systems demanding new and improved uses of various metals and alloys
- the invention of the automobile and the subsequent production of untold billions of components for the cars, trucks, and other vehicles that have been produced in the last century
- the growth of large cities and the tall buildings made necessary by limitations in available building space
- the expansion of modern highway systems, including thousands of bridges ranging from small structures to giant bridges such as the Golden Gate Bridge
- recent advances in the air and space industry, the development of nuclear power plants, and other high-tech industries in which metalworkers have faced new challenges and opportunities.

WHY PURSUE A METALWORKING CAREER?

Why might anyone pursue a career in a metalworking field? Here are several possible benefits:

Attractive wages. In general, men and women employed in metalworking jobs earn attractive wages and benefits. Their jobs require special skills, and employers are willing to pay wages reflecting the particular knowledge and skills involved. In the more complex positions, workers may earn several times the average pay received by unskilled workers. In addition, metalworkers often receive substantial fringe benefits. These benefits may include pension plans, health insurance, medical insurance, educational pay, and other valuable support.

Job satisfaction. A good job should offer more than just good wages. It should also prove interesting. Many people find that metalworking jobs challenge them to learn new skills and then apply them in the process of construction, repair, or other workplace efforts.

Unfortunately, many workers in what are often called unskilled jobs find little satisfaction in their work. Many such jobs in agriculture, service industries, and other areas require no special training or abilities, thus virtually anyone can perform them. However, they usually pay low wages and often consist of boring, repetitive work.

Most jobs in metalworking, on the other hand, are different. They can be done only by people who have mastered certain basic techniques and who in many cases have completed special training. As a result, workers who have developed such specialized capabilities can experience justifiable compensation and self-confidence. And perhaps even more important, the end result is often a product of which the worker can be proud. The act of building or repairing something can be extremely rewarding. One of the nicest feelings in life is to step back and take a long look at a building, bridge, or piece of equipment that *you* have built or helped construct. Persons employed in metalworking usually can enjoy the intangible benefits of such accomplishments.

Potential for the future. When you choose a career, how do you know that there will still be a demand for that kind of work ten years or more into the future? After all, we live in an increasingly changing world. New inventions and entire new industries seem to spring up overnight, and workers are sometimes lost in the transition.

It would be misleading to say that this will never happen in any given technical field, for no one can predict the future with any real degree of accuracy. But the future in many metalworking jobs seems solid. The need for trained metalworkers is expected to continue far into the future, despite the increased use of plastics, ceramics, and other products. Changing technology is unlikely to eliminate the use of metal, but rather prompt new ways of using different metals in combination with other materials.

A suitable work environment. Do you want to spend your working life seated behind a desk in an air-conditioned office? If so, a metalworking job may not be for you. On the other hand, if you would prefer working with your hands in an active and potentially varied environment, perhaps working as a machinist, welder, or other metalworker will be just right for you.

This working environment may consist of a workbench in a small business, the floor of a large factory, the unfinished portion of a bridge or skyscraper, or any number of other settings. It may be indoors or out. Some jobs will involve going from one construction site to the next as projects are completed. Others may be on the production line of a huge plant or in the workroom of a small one. In any case, the surroundings and the type of work undertaken may be well suited to your own particular idea of an appropriate workplace.

Job opportunities without four years of college. You don't need a bachelor's degree to pursue a career in metalworking. Instead, you can participate in on-the-job training or an apprenticeship, or enroll in a program taking anywhere from a few months to two years to complete, depending on the field involved and the type of training followed.

In some cases, you can go straight from high school to a metalworking job. In others, a comprehensive training effort will be needed. But in either situation, you can find yourself in a well-paying job while friends and acquaintances are still in their third or fourth year of postsecondary education.

Geographical flexibility. Jobs in various metalworking fields can be found throughout the United States, Canada, and many other countries. Of course more positions can be expected in urban areas than rural ones, but there are no special geographical limitations for careers in this field.

This flexibility often can mean finding a good job without having to leave the area where you now live, if that is your preference. If you hope to move to new locations, metalworking skills can be a great asset for helping you find employment in a new area. Because of the widespread use of metal for so many purposes, job possibilities in the various related fields can be found virtually anywhere.

EXPLORING FURTHER

Want to know more? The following chapters cover various fields within the overall career area of metalworking, along with tips on breaking into the field of your choice and what you can expect if you become employed in this area. Chapter 2 provides an overview of the major metalworking fields. Chapter 3 covers sheet-metal working, while machining and machine operation are covered in Chapter 4. Chapter 5 looks at structural and reinforcing metalworking, and Chapter 6 provides an introduction to welding. Chapter 7 covers the jewelry making field.

A look at the educational work needed to prepare for a metalworking career appears in Chapter 8. This chapter also provides tips for doing well in training programs. Chapter 9 discusses earnings and fringe benefits. Approaches to breaking into a metalworking field are covered in Chapter 10. The book also includes several appendices, including a list of schools providing appropriate training programs.

Perhaps a career in metalworking holds promise for you. Take a look at the information provided, and you may find yourself on the way to a promising and worthwhile career.

CHAPTER 2

METALWORKING: A DIVERSE TECHNOLOGY

Even though metalworking is a technology that has existed for thousands of years, it remains one of the most vital aspects of modern life. Methods of working with metal include both traditional practices perfected over the centuries and exciting new techniques developed in today's age of computers and sophisticated industrial applications.

THE EXPANSIVE NATURE OF METALWORKING

Persons who work with metal hold a wide variety of jobs. Most of them can be grouped into the following major fields:

- sheet-metal working
- machining and machine operation
- structural and reinforcing metalworking
- welding
- jewelry making

A brief description of each field follows. Additional details for these occupations are provided in subsequent chapters.

Sheet-Metal Working

Sheet-metal workers make, install, or repair items with sheet metal. They are employed throughout the United States and Canada in a variety of industries. Many of them work in building construction, where they construct hangars, storage buildings, or other structures. Others may install aluminum siding, skylights, roofs, or outdoor signs. Still others work with air-conditioning, heating, or ventilation systems. This work may include fabricating, installing, or repairing air ducts in homes, office buildings, or other structures.

Persons employed in this field sometimes specialize in a specific task, such as installing rain gutters or aluminum siding. They work for various types of employers including large construction companies, smaller firms, and specialized companies providing air-conditioning and heating services. Depending on the type of work being conducted, they may work primarily with hand tools or may use automated equipment.

Machining and Machine Operation

Machinists and machine operators produce precision parts of metal, or sometimes plastic, for a wide range of uses. The items they produce usually must meet very detailed specifications for size, shape, and other characteristics. For example, machinists and related workers may make parts for airplanes, automobiles, or industrial machinery.

Machinists are highly skilled workers. The main distinction between machinists and machine operators is that machinists concentrate on making or repairing items that must be produced individually or in small quantities, as opposed to those made through assembly lines or other mass production processes. Machine operators, on the other hand, usually produce items in larger quantities where mass production is the goal.

Machinists may work with a wide range of metals including steel, copper, iron, aluminum, and various alloys. The work often involves building or adjusting parts of equipment that must meet specific requirements for size, configuration, or other characteristics. Machinists may build new parts from printed designs, duplicate parts, develop variations of existing items, or make precision repairs.

Machine operators concentrate on high-volume production. They often work in manufacturing plants where they produce items such as parts for various types of equipment and consumer goods.

Structural and Reinforcing Metalworking

Workers in this field are most commonly referred to as ironworkers. Their jobs usually consist of assembling the steel or iron frameworks of bridges, buildings, and other large structures. Ironworkers install metal bars, rods, beams, columns, and other components. They may build the internal structure around which a multistory office building is erected, put together reinforcing for a concrete retaining wall, or install steel fire escapes or stairs, among other duties.

This work often involves lifting and positioning steel beams and similar items through the use of derricks or cranes. A typical job might include setting up such equipment, unloading and stacking steel beams, and then hoisting them high into the air as part of a major construction project.

Ironworkers hold jobs across the United States and Canada wherever construction projects are under way. They are more likely to find jobs in growing urban areas.

Welding

Welders join metals together using heat or other special processes. They work in a variety of industries including the construction of ships, airplanes, and automobiles. They also join steel rods and beams in highways, bridges, buildings, and other heavy construction.

Welders may perform any of several basic processes. In electric arc welding, an electric current creates heat as it arcs between the tip of a welding electrode and metal. In gas welding, heat formed by burning gases is used to melt metal and cause it to fuse. In resistance welding, electric current flows through weld metal and heats it. Some welders may perform new types of welding that utilize laser beams or electron beams.

Some persons employed in this field master a variety of welding processes, while others concentrate on a single technique or welding application. Welding jobs in heavy construction or repair of machines and equipment may require specialized skills, but some positions consist of working on an assembly line and using welding machines that make the operator's job less complex.

Welders find a demand for their skills in large corporations, small companies, and a variety of geographical locations throughout North America.

Jewelry Making

Not all metalworking jobs involve construction or heavy manufacturing. The field of making or repairing jewelry offers a different range of opportunities.

Jewelers and related workers perform highly skilled and detailed work. They produce or repair varying types of jewelry such as rings, brooches, bracelets, earrings, and necklaces. This work may include working with precious metals such as gold and silver as well as other valuable materials including diamonds and precious and semiprecious gems.

Jewelers may work in manufacturing facilities that specialize in the production of jewelry, in department stores, or in small retail stores. Their work might include anything from assembling a set of earrings to repairing the broken clasp of a necklace. In some instances, their work may cross into other areas such as customer relations or business management.

Because of society's continuing demand for beautiful jewelry, a continuing demand also exists for persons to work in this area. The jewelry making field offers long-term potential for persons who can perform the precise and sometimes creative work required.

WIDE-RANGING JOB POSSIBILITIES

Metalworking offers a great deal of diversity. A career in this area might take you to the top of a forty-story building where huge steel beams are being hoisted about. Or it might involve sitting at a workbench assembling a necklace, or refining a precision part of a piece of industrial equipment. Such diversity means that many options await the person who hopes to pursue a career in one of these interesting fields.

CHAPTER 3

SHEET-METAL WORKING

A common application of metalworking technology is forming it into sheets that can then be used in building all kinds of products. Those who work with this process may be known by a variety of job titles, but the most common overall term is simply sheet-metal workers.

Men and women employed as sheet-metal workers perform work such as the following:

- fabricating or installing ducts for air-conditioning systems, heating units, and ventilation systems
- forming and installing rain gutters on houses or other buildings
- installing aluminum siding on residences and office buildings
- making and installing outdoor signs
- repairing various structures made of sheet metal

Such tasks often include a combination of functions. Sheet-metal workers may assemble items, install them, or do both. They also may provide maintenance and repair services. The

Dictionary of Occupational Titles provides this job description of a sheet-metal worker:

> Plans, lays out, fabricates, assembles, installs, and repairs sheet metal parts, equipment, and products, utilizing knowledge of working characteristics of metallic and nonmetallic materials, machining, and layout techniques, using handtools, power tools, machines, and equipment: Reads and interprets blueprints, sketches, or product specifications to determine sequence and methods of fabricating, assembling, and installing sheet metal products. Selects gauge and type of sheet metal, such as galvanized iron, copper, steel, or aluminum, or nonmetallic material, such as plastics or fiberglass, according to product specifications. Lays out and marks dimensions and reference lines on material, using scribers, dividers, squares, and rulers, applying knowledge of shop mathematics and layout techniques to develop and trace patterns of product or parts...or using templates. Sets up and operates fabricating machines, such as shears, brakes, presses, forming rolls, and routers, to cut, bend, block and form, or straighten materials. Shapes metal material over anvil, block, or other form, using handtools. Trims, files, grinds, deburrs, buffs, and smooths surfaces, using handtools and portable power tools. Welds, solders, bolts, rivets, screws, clips, caulks, or bonds component parts to assemble products, using handtools, power tools, and equipment. Installs assemblies in supportive framework according to blueprints, using handtools, power tools, and lifting and handling devices. Inspects assemblies and installation for conformance to specifications, using mea-

suring instruments, such as calipers, scales, dial indicators, gauges, and micrometers. Repairs and maintains sheet metal products. May operate computer-aided-drafting (CAD) equipment to develop scale drawings of product or system. May operate laser-beam cutter…or plasma arc cutter…to cut patterns from sheet metal.

JOB TITLES

Many persons employed in this field hold specialized positions in which they perform specific types of sheet-metal work. Representative job titles listed by the U.S. Department of Labor in this area include the following:

Assembler, Production Line
Assembler, Unit
Channel Installer
Door-Lock Installer
Fabricator, Shower Doors and Panels
Fireproof-Door Assembler
Frame Assembler
Hardware Installer
Inspector and Tester
Kick-Plate Installer
Measurer
Metal-Door Assembler
Metal Screen, Storm Door, and Window Builder

Metal Window-Screen Assembler
Ornamental-Metalwork Designer
Ornamental-Metalworker
Screen-Frame Enameler
Screen Installer
Scroll-Machine Operator
Shop Supervisor
Supervisor, Assembly Department
Supervisor, Grinding and Spraying

WORK PERFORMED

For an example of work performed in this field, consider a typical day put in by Roberto, who works for a growing business specializing in heating and air-conditioning systems. His latest job consists of installing such a system in a new building designed to house an auto repair shop. Not only will the comfort of workers and customers depend on the new system, but safety also will be a key factor: the job will include placing exhaust ducts in several locations so that carbon monoxide and other harmful gases will not accumulate within the building.

To get started, Roberto reviews blueprints that have been provided by his supervisor. Working inside a shop at the company's downtown location, he begins assembling ducts by using computerized equipment purchased recently by his company. This includes a saw that cuts metal according to preprogrammed instructions that Roberto enters electronically. After the ducts have been assembled, Roberto travels by truck to the site of the new building, where he uses hand tools to put the ducts in place. He fastens pieces together and then inspects the system to make sure all parts fit together properly. If necessary, he will make adjustments on site or take materials back to the shop for revision.

In this particular case, the job will take slightly more than one day to complete. Roberto will work an eight-hour day, taking time off for lunch and two short breaks, and at the end of the day will clean up the area where he has worked, store tools in the truck, and return to the shop for a new assignment.

Specific tasks performed by Roberto or other sheet-metal workers may include:

- using rulers, tapes, or other similar devices to measure material
- planning layouts for installation projects
- making calculations by hand or with electronic calculators
- using small hand tools such as hammers, drills, snips, and hacksaws
- operating welding machines or soldering equipment
- operating computer-controlled saws, presses, or other high-tech equipment
- installing systems and metal parts at sites away from the shop or place of employment
- altering or repairing structures constructed of sheet metal

- cutting large metal sheets into smaller pieces
- fastening materials together with bolts, screws, clips, rivets, or other items
- checking the size and shape of metal parts for a good fit
- testing or adjusting completed projects
- making cost estimates
- ordering or purchasing materials
- transporting materials and equipment to job sites
- communicating with customers and coworkers

Job duties can vary widely within this field. One person may spend all of his or her time assembling products of the same type, such as tops for pick-up trucks or home storage buildings. Another may perform different types of tasks depending upon the needs of each customer or varying assignments from a supervisor.

In working with sheet metal, the overall situation for any one individual may be quite different from that of another. At the same time, the similarity in basic skills used means that workers in this field can sometimes switch from one type of work to another rather easily, until they find the situation they like best.

WORKING CONDITIONS

One of the advantages of many jobs in the sheet-metal field is that they provide variety in work settings. A job installing heating and air-conditioning ducts, for example, might take an individual to a wide range of different locations. A week or more might be spent at a large office building, followed by a day's work at a private residence. During the course of a year, some workers might experience dozens or even hundreds of changes in work settings. This can be an asset for people who become bored easily and thrive on change.

Not all jobs in the field provide such a degree of change. Some positions involve working in a shop or factory where sheet-metal products are manufactured or assembled. Workers in these kinds of positions show up at the same location every day and encounter relatively little change in working environment. This can be an advantage or disadvantage, depending on personal preferences.

Sheet-metal workers often perform their work outdoors. This can mean enjoying the pleasure of a sunny spring day or suffering the discomfort of winter winds or summer heat. Indoor situations also can be uncomfortable at times—for example, working in a building that has not yet had heating or air-conditioning installed. Workers who encounter such situations learn to compensate by wearing appropriate clothing.

SKILLS NEEDED TO SUCCEED

Few special skills are absolutely necessary for any person to have the potential to become a sheet-metal worker. Most of the techniques involved can be learned by anyone who has reasonably good hand-to-eye coordination and a basic ability to work with tools. In addition, it helps to have most or all of the following traits:

1. *An aptitude for working with mechanical devices.* This might be indicated by aptitude tests as well as past experiences. A person who is good at working on cars, doing carpentry, or repairing household appliances, for instance, probably can learn the basics of sheet-metal working very readily. However, someone who has had no experience in any related activities might nevertheless have the necessary potential.

2. *Physical dexterity.* The nature of most work in this field requires nimble hands and fingers. A lack of physical strength can perhaps be offset by other skills, but it would be difficult to perform without being able to use one's hands efficiently. Also, the ability to climb, crawl, and otherwise move about would be an asset.

3. *Stamina.* Persons working with sheet metal may spend all day on their feet in different types of settings, such as a shop with a concrete floor or outdoors during cold weather. The stamina to undertake such work is a necessary commodity.

4. *Pride in work skills.* To succeed on a long-term basis, a certain element of pride in doing a good job is needed. This means caring enough to take extra time

if needed, or redoing a piece of work that is not up to par. Sheet-metal work requires an eye for precision and a positive working attitude.

LEARNING THE TRADE

There are a number of ways to learn the basics of sheet-metal working. You do not need to attend college to break into the field, although a high school diploma may be required.

Some vocational schools at the high school level teach basic skills that can be applied to the tasks performed by sheet-metal workers. Still other skills can be learned on your own as you work in a home shop or other setting. In addition, some nonunion employers will hire inexperienced men and women and then train them on the job in an informal fashion.

A more organized and comprehensive approach is to sign up for an apprenticeship program. Such programs are sponsored by the Sheet Metal Workers' International Association (a major union for workers in this field) and the Air Conditioning Contractors' National Association. They combine work experience and classroom training, normally spread over a four-year period.

According to "Careers in Sheet Metal," a publication of the National Training Fund for the Sheet Metal and Air Conditioning Industry, persons who complete a formal apprenticeship program of this type sign an agreement that stipulates their responsibilities and rights under the program. They then complete at least four years of on-the-job training—about eight thousand working hours—as well as additional time in class. More details about formal apprenticeship programs are provided in Chapter 8.

QUESTIONS TO ASK YOURSELF

The National Training Fund for the Sheet Metal and Air Conditioning Industry suggests you ask yourself these questions if you are considering a career as a sheet-metal worker:

1. Have you finished or are you about to finish high school?
2. Did you do well in your math course(s)?
3. Did you take drafting and enjoy it?
4. Do you like shop work and doing things with your hands?
5. Are you willing to work and also go to school?
6. Are you healthy, with no major disability and no fear of heights or climbing?
7. Would you be willing to work outdoors in varying weather conditions as well as indoors?
8. Are you willing to serve four years of apprenticeship in the sheet-metal industry?

9. Are you willing to get your hands dirty?
10. Would you like to be a skilled union sheet-metal worker?

It is not necessary to answer "yes" to all these questions, but anyone with seven or more positive responses should have good prospects for success in this field, according to the Training Fund. Of course, questions about apprenticeships and union membership may not apply in a nonunion setting, but the other questions should have applicability in most areas of the sheet-metal field. If you consider them carefully and can answer in the affirmative to most of them, a sheet-metal career may be worth exploring further.

CHAPTER 4

MACHINING AND MACHINE OPERATION

A challenging area of the metalworking industry is machining. This involves the production of metal parts, many of them small and precise, for various uses. Machinists make or repair precision parts that must be produced individually or in small quantities rather than through an assembly line or other automated process. Machine operators, on the other hand, perform related work but on a different scale. They operate machines that produce equipment parts or other devices, often in large quantities.

Both types of jobs offer a wide range of opportunities. Because their work is so basic to any manufacturing process, persons with the right skills in this area are often in great demand in a variety of industries.

WORK OF MACHINISTS

Machinists produce various items made of iron, steel, brass, aluminum, and other metals. In most cases, these items must conform to specifications provided to them with each particular task assigned. For example, a machinist may build a component of a printing press, airplane engine, industrial machine, or other piece of equipment. This may involve developing a new part "from scratch" or duplicating one that has become worn out or broken.

In producing such items, machinists may perform such tasks as the following:

- reading blueprints or other written specifications
- taking precise measurements
- selecting appropriate metal stock
- planning steps for completing a job, from cutting the initial shape to finishing or polishing the surface
- making mathematical calculations by hand or with a calculator
- operating equipment such as drills, grinders, and lathes
- using various types of equipment to cut, drill, or otherwise shape items being manufactured or modified
- operating automated equipment such as numerical control equipment
- writing or adapting computer programs for numerical control equipment
- finishing and assembling machined components
- testing and adjusting parts that have been manufactured

Because of the precise nature of their work, machinists typically work slowly and methodically. They often earn a great deal of respect from other workers because their work is seen as highly skilled and crucial to the manufacturing process. A commitment to high quality is often a major mode of operation in the machine shop setting.

An especially interesting aspect of machinists' work is that it is becoming increasingly automated. The advent of computer-controlled equipment has allowed machinists to become more productive than ever and has added a fascinating element to this career area.

WORK OF MACHINE OPERATORS

Although related to machinists, machine operators generally represent a separate category of workers. A major difference is that they tend to concentrate on high-volume production rather than the small quantities dealt with by machinists.

The *Dictionary of Occupational Titles* provides the following description of the work of a machine operator, emphasizing the fabrication process:

> Sets up and operates machine tools, such as lathes, milling machines, boring machines, and grinders, to machine metallic and nonmetallic workpieces according to specifications, tooling instructions, and standard charts, applying knowledge of machining methods: Reads blueprint or job order for product specifications, such as dimensions and tolerances, and tooling instructions, such as fixtures, feed rates, cutting speeds, depth of cut, and determines sequence of operations. Selects, positions, and secures tool in tool-

holder (chuck, collet, or toolpost). Positions and secures workpiece in holding device, machine table, chuck, centers, or fixtures, using clamps and wrenches. Moves controls to position tool and work-piece in relation to each other, and to set specified feeds, speeds, and depth of cut. Sets up fixture or feeding device, starts machine, and turns handwheel to feed tool to workpiece or vice versa, and engages feed. Turns valve handle to direct flow of coolant or cutting oil against tool and workpiece. Observes oper-ation of machine and verifies conformance of machined workpiece to specifications, using measur-ing instruments, such as fixed gauges, calipers, and micrometers. Operates bench grinder to sharpen tools. May set up and operate machines and equipment other than machine tools, such as welding machines and flame-cutting equipment.

With the increased use of plastics in manufacturing, this area of metalworking also may include working with plas-tics. Some people employed in the field work with both metal and plastic, while others work only with one of the two materials.

A major employer in this field is the automotive industry. Many workers are needed to produce the large quantities of parts needed in the production of motor vehicles. Large numbers of workers also are employed in the mass produc-tion of fabricated metal products, primary metal products, electrical and electronic equipment, and machinery.

Machine operators often specialize in running one or two types of equipment. For example, workers may operate a machine that produces ball bearings or coats a metal machine component with another type of metal. Their responsibilities may include feeding materials through the equipment, monitoring factors such as volume and temperature, and observing safety standards necessary in using automated equipment.

JOB TITLES

Among the job titles listed in the *Dictionary of Occupational Titles* in machining and related areas are:

Carbide-Die Maker
Diamond-Die Maker
Die Barber
Die Designer
Die Finisher
Drill-Press Operator
Drill Sharpener
Engine Lathe Operator, Numerical Control
Gear-Cutting-Machine Operator
Grinder, Gear
Grinder, Machine
Machine Set-Up Operator
Machinist
Machinist Apprentice
Machinist, Experimental

Milling Machine Operator
Mold Stamper
Numerical-Control-Machine Operator
Reamer Operator
Screw-Machine Operator
Surface Grinding Machine Operator
Template Maker, Extrusion Die
Tool-and-Die Maker
Tool Repairer
Valve Grinder

These are representative of the field but are by no means inclusive; all told, more than 250 job titles can be found in this area.

TRAINING OPTIONS

Persons who want to learn machining or machine operations can choose from several types of training. In some cases, this can be obtained on the job when an employer is willing to hire an untrained person and allow the individual to learn from other workers while conducting actual work for the company. This is the norm in machine operations, which in most settings is considered a less advanced skill than machining itself. Sometimes on-the-job training is also possible in machining.

For machinists, entry into the field is usually based on completing a formal training program. This may be an apprenticeship program, not unlike that followed by sheet-metal workers but focusing on different skills. Or it might mean attending a vocational school, trade school, or two-year college. Chapter 8 covers these options in more detail.

Some of the more advanced machining skills can be learned in community, junior, or technical colleges. Many colleges across North America offer programs in this area. Men and women who enroll in such programs study a comprehensive array of techniques and background information. For example, students at Central Piedmont Community College in Charlotte, North Carolina, may earn a Machinist Diploma by completing a program of courses including the following:

- Precision Instrument Reading
- Fundamentals of Computer Numerical Control Programming
- Blueprint Reading for Machinists I and II
- Basic Lathe Operations
- Calculations for Machinists
- Basic Milling Operations
- Computer Numerical Control Programming (several specialized courses)
- Layout, Hand Tool, and Drill Press Procedures
- Grinding Machine Operations
- Applied Metallurgy I and II

- Applied Physics I and II
- Basic Oxyacetylene Welding

After successfully completing these and related courses, students earn a diploma that qualifies them for jobs in industry.

Students at Iowa's Kirkwood Community College can earn an associate degree in CNC Manufacturing Technology, which includes advanced courses in computer numerical control. This program takes two years (four semesters and one summer) of full-time study. Students in the associate degree program learn to program, edit, set up, and operate lathes and mills that are controlled by computers. They also learn quality control methods such as statistical process control, how to operate special equipment such as data collectors and coordinate measuring machines, and the basics of factory automation.

At New River Community College in Dublin, Virginia, students pursue a two-year program that culminates in an associate degree. The program prepares graduates for jobs such as:

Inspector (quality control)
Machine Shop Supervisor
Machinist
Methods Technician
Planning Technician

Following is a description of some of the courses offered in this program:

MAC 105. *Machine Shop Operations* (nine credits). Teaches bench work, sawing, drilling, lathe, milling, grinding, and use of precision measuring instruments and safety. Lecture 4 hours, laboratory 15 hours, total 19 hours per week.

MAC 109. *Machine Shop Practices* (nine credits). Offers practice in bench work, sawing, drilling, lathe, milling, grinding, and precision measuring instruments. May require solutions of related problems and preparation of weekly laboratory reports. Lecture 4 hours, laboratory 15 hours, total 19 hours per week.

MAC 121-122. *Numerical Control I and II* (nine credits). Focuses on numerical control techniqes in metal-forming and machine processes. Includes theory and practice in lathe and milling machine computer numerical control program writing, setup, and operation. Lecture 3 hours, laboratory 3 hours, total 6 hours per week.

MAC 131-132. *Machine Lab I and II.* (Two separate courses, two credits each.) Teaches fundamental machine shop operations, bench work, layout, measuring tools, and safety. Lecture 1 hour, laboratory 3 hours, total 4 hours per week.

MAC 181-182. *Machine Blueprint Reading I and II.* (Two courses, three credits each.) Introduces reading and interpreting blueprints and working drawings. Applies visualization of objects, sketching, and machine terminology. Lecture 3 hours per week.

MAC 215. *Machining Techniques* (nine credits). Teaches milling lathe operations, precision grinding, production tooling, and machine tool attachments.

Lecture 4 hours, laboratory 15 hours, total 19 hours per week.

MAC 217. *Precision Machining Techniques* (nine credits). Teaches precision layout, machining techniques, high-precision grinding, measuring tool calibration, and inspection procedures. Lecture 4 hours, laboratory 15 hours, total 19 hours per week.

In addition to the courses in machine technology, students must complete courses in technical mathematics, a technical writing course, an orientation to college, and a few other courses outside the field.

One of the most useful features of the better schools is that they maintain close ties with local industries. Typically, this includes regular meetings between faculty and members of an advisory committee made up of machinists, supervisors, owners of small shops, and managers in larger manufacturing firms. They not only help make certain the college teaches its students the right skills, but also often strengthen chances for graduates to land good jobs after completing their training.

WORKING ENVIRONMENT

Unlike some other related fields, machining and machine operations seldom involve outdoor work. Instead, most work is performed in shops or factories. This means that the daily working environment will not provide a great deal of variety, but workers are spared the discomfort of adapting to weather conditions.

Machinists may work in a small shop setting or in a larger factory. Good lighting and ventilation are the norm.

Machine operators often work on assembly lines in large factories. Such settings may be noisy, poorly lit, and crowded. This is not always the case, however, especially in more modern facilities.

In both types of jobs, workers may need to wear special safety equipment such as goggles, earplugs, or protective shoes. They may also need to avoid wearing loose-fitting clothing or jewelry that could become caught in equipment.

CHAPTER 5

STRUCTURAL AND REINFORCING METALWORKING

Some of the most important work with metals is per-formed by structural and reinforcing metal workers. These workers, also known as ironworkers, play a central role in the construction industry by erecting the framework around which other parts of structures are built. Ironworkers build the steel frameworks of large buildings. They perform simi-lar functions in the construction of bridges. They also pro-vide reinforcing for concrete structures, install metal components of buildings such as steel stairs and walls, work with equipment for hoisting and lifting metal, and perform related work.

A simple way to view the role of ironworkers is to com-pare their efforts with those performed by sheet-metal work-ers as discussed in Chapter 3. Whereas sheet-metal workers tend to deal with the outer "skin" of structures, structural and reinforcing metal workers concentrate more on their "skeletons." Just as the skeleton of a human body supports the rest of its anatomy, the metal beams, rods, bars, and other parts assembled by ironworkers form the internal framework for buildings and other structures.

The *Dictionary of Occupational Titles* provides this job description for an ironworker:

> Performs any combination of following duties to raise, place, and unite girders, columns, and other structural-steel members to form completed structures or structure frameworks, working as member of crew: Sets up hoisting equipment for raising and placing structural-steel members. Fastens steel members to cable of hoist, using chain, cable, or rope. Signals worker operating hoisting equipment to lift and place steel member. Guides member, using tab line (rope) or rides on member in order to guide it into position. Pulls, pushes, or pries steel members into approximate position while member is supported by hoisting device. Forces members into final position, using turnbuckles, crowbars, jacks, and handtools. Aligns rivet holes in member with corresponding holes in previously placed member by driving drift pins or handle of wrench through holes. Verifies vertical and horizontal alignment of members, using plumb bob and level. Bolts aligned members to keep them into position until they can be permanently riveted, bolted, or welded in place. Catches hot rivets tossed by RIVET HEATER (heat treating) in bucket and inserts rivets in holes, using tongs. Bucks (holds) rivets while RIVETER, PNEUMATIC (any industry) uses air hammer to form heads on rivets. Cuts and welds steel members to make alterations, using oxyacetylene welding equipment.

JOBS PERFORMED

Typical jobs performed by ironworkers may include the following:

- setting up cranes and derricks used to lift building materials high into the air for construction of a multistory office building
- unloading steel beams from a truck and stacking them for later use in building a bridge
- attaching a cable from a crane to a steel girder so it can be hoisted into position
- reading blueprints in preparation for building a steel water tower
- using bolts and hand tools to connect beams that will support the walls of a new warehouse
- welding steel rods together to help form the roof for a new bank building
- positioning rods to form reinforcing for a floor that will be made of concrete
- installing a metal fire escape on the outside of a large apartment building
- assembling a storage tank for heating oil at a factory
- putting together the metal portions of a steel-and-concrete bridge

Additional specific tasks performed by ironworkers can include:

- setting steel bars in place to reinforce concrete
- cutting and fitting wire mesh for concrete reinforcement
- unloading and stacking steel beams or other materials
- bolting together girders, beams, or columns
- setting up cables for hoisting equipment
- using hand signals to direct hoist operators
- assisting in hoisting beams or other materials above the ground
- using various hand tools to position, fasten, or cut pieces of metal
- operating laser alignment equipment
- welding metal structures or portions of structures together
- repairing metal structures
- installing metal window frames
- installing metal stairways
- assembling ornamental enhancements to buildings
- erecting industrial storage tanks

As with other metalworking fields, much variety can be found from one type of job to the next. Many ironworkers, however, specialize in one type of work. For example, one person may work mostly in the construction of large buildings. Another may specialize in ornamental metalwork. Still another may work primarily in road and bridge construction.

Most ironworkers are employed by large construction companies. Unlike machining or sheet-metal work, relatively few small businesses exist in this field due to the large amounts of money required for equipment as well as materials such as steel beams.

The majority of jobs can be found in large and medium-sized cities. Some ironworkers relocate to find work or are sent long distances by their employers, but this is not necessarily a requirement.

WORKING ENVIRONMENT

By the very nature of their jobs, most structural and reinforcing metalworkers must spend a great deal of time outdoors. Often, the part of the structure they are building must be completed before walls or roofs are installed, thus exposing workers to the vagaries of weather conditions. These can vary according to location and season. Hot summer days can impose an unavoidable degree of discomfort, as can wind and rain. In many parts of North America, workers also must face cold weather for at least part of the year, including snow, sleet, and subfreezing temperatures. Such conditions not only affect individual comfort, but also restrict working schedules. Bad weather can delay completion of projects and result in lost working days.

Working conditions for ironworkers often involve the additional factor of height. Many jobs in this field require working high above the ground. The most graphic example of this element of the job might be the construction of a huge office building in a large city. In such a setting, a worker might be perched sixty stories or more above the ground, walking across narrow beams. But even working a few feet above the ground poses special safety requirements as well as the mental or psychological ability to cope with such settings.

SKILLS NEEDED FOR SUCCESS

The skills necessary for working as an ironworker can be acquired by both men and women who have the necessary basic traits upon which to build.

First among these traits are basic manual skills. Ironworkers must use tools and apply a basic understanding of mechanical principles; thus you should have an aptitude for such things, even if you have not learned a great deal about the details of using various tools. Do you enjoy working with your hands? Do you have a good eye for detail? Does the idea of working as an ironworker seem to match the way you see yourself in the world of work? A positive answer to these questions would help for a career in this field to become a reality.

Another basic trait needed is physical fitness. Working in this field often involves hard, physical labor. You must be physically fit to succeed. This does not mean you must have bulging muscles or be a large person; after all, the really heavy lifting may be handled by machines. But at the same time, some degree of strength is needed. Agility, stamina, and the ability to work at substantial heights above the ground, if necessary, also will be assets.

Finally, anyone who works in this field should be highly conscious of safety, or at least have the capacity for developing such a trait. Constant attention to this factor is needed to avoid falls or other accidents.

TRAINING OPTIONS

Most ironworkers acquire their skills on the job or through an apprenticeship. A high school diploma may be needed, but it is not necessary to attend college to break into this field.

If you seek a position in which the employer will provide on-the-job training, your case will be strengthened if you have taken vocational courses in high school. Or if you can demonstrate an aptitude for working with tools and a willingness to learn, you may have an edge over other applicants.

Probably the best way to pursue a career as an ironworker is to complete a formal apprenticeship. Such opportunities are provided by the International Association of Bridge, Structural and Ornamental Ironworkers in cooperation with contractors who employ workers. Completion of an apprenticeship requires three years of on-the-job training plus at least 144 hours of classroom study each year.

Subjects studied during an apprenticeship include:

- use of tools
- material properties and handling
- basic math applications
- safety procedures
- structural erecting
- rigging
- welding
- ornamental assembling

In addition to these subjects, apprentices gain experience on the job in the various tasks expected of full-fledged workers. Generally, they develop greater independence as time passes and their skill levels grow. Additional information about training options is provided in Chapter 8.

CHAPTER 6

WELDING

Another important type of metalworking is welding. In welding, workers join two or more pieces of metal (or sometimes other materials) through use of heat, pressure, or a related process. The result is that the metals become fused together.

Welders help build automobiles, ships, airplanes, buildings, bridges, appliances, and many other items made in whole or part of metal. They also may repair metallic items. To do such work, welders use special equipment and apply job-specific knowledge. Because their work is needed in a variety of industries, men and women who can perform welding functions continue to enjoy demand for their services throughout the United States and Canada.

WELDING PROCESSES

Although it has existed for more than a century, welding is a field that keeps changing with new technological developments. Welding was first developed in the 1880s in Europe and America. Over the years, experts in the field have developed a wide range of welding processes. Today's welding techniques include the following:

Gas welding. This is one of the most basic types of welding. A special torch is used to burn acetylene or another flammable gas, which produces a flame hot enough to melt metal. In its basic form, gas welding involves the use of a handheld torch operated by a single individual.

Arc welding. In this welding process, high temperatures are generated by an electric arc instead of burning gases. In most cases, a generator is employed to produce electric current, which is then used to create the arc that jumps between the metal surface and the welder's tool—either an electrode or a welding rod. Arc welding can be a simple, one-person task or a complex, automated process.

Resistance welding. This process is different from arc welding in that instead of an arc, the flow of electricity between two pieces of metal creates resistance, and they become fused together.

Advanced technologies. Other types of welding are based on recent high-tech advancements. For example, some advanced types of welding involve the use of sound waves, lasers, or electron beams.

JOB TITLES

Welding is a diverse field. Following are just some of the job titles related to welding listed by the U.S. Department of Labor:

Arc Cutter

Gas-Tungsten Arc Cutter

Plasma Arc Cutter

Brazer

Crawler Torch Brazer

Electronic Brazer

Furnace Brazer

Furnace Brazer Helper

Induction Brazer Helper

Induction Brazer

Production Line Brazer

Repair and Salvage Brazer

Resistance Brazer

Brazing-Furnace Feeder

Brazer-Machine Feeder

Brazing-Machine Operator

Hand Burner

Burning-Machine Operator

Certified Welder

Gas Cutter

Electronic-Eye-Thermal-Cutting-Machine Operator

Flame-Brazing-Machine Operator

Flame-Cutting-Machine Operator

Flame-Cutting-Machine-Operator Helper

Flame Gouger

Flame Planer

Flame Scarfer

Flash-Welding-Machine Operator

Flash Brusher
Gas-Cutting-Machine Operator
Hydrogen Braze-Furnace Operator
Laser-Beam Cutter
Laser-Beam-Machine Operator
Lead Burner
Lead-Burner Apprentice
Lead-Burner Supervisor
Machine Feeder
Machine Helper
Magnetic-Thermal-Cutting-Machine Operator
Percussion-Welding-Machine Operator
Performance-Test Inspector
Plasma-Cutting-Machine Operator
Production-Welding-Machine Operator
Cylinder Heads Repairer
Welding Equipment Repairer
Induction-Heating-Equipment Setter
Solderer-Assembler
Solderer-Dipper
Electronic Solderer
Furnace Solderer
Induction Solderer
Production Line Solderer
Silver Solderer
Torch Solderer
Soldering-Machine Feeder

Soldering-Machine Operator
Soldering-Machine Operator Helper
Hand Thermal Cutter
Thermal-Cutter Helper
Thermal-Cutting-Tracer-Machine Operator
Torch Brazer
Torch Cutter
Upset-Welding-Machine Operator
Acetylene Welder
Arc Welder Apprentice
Arc Welder
Gas Welder
Gas Welder Apprentice
Combination Welder
Combination Welder Apprentice
Experimental Welder
Explosion Welder
Welder-Fitter
Welder-Fitter Apprentice
Arc Welder-Fitter
Gas Welder-Fitter
Flux-Cored Arc Welder
Gas-Metal Arc Welder
Gas-Tungsten Arc Welder
Gun Welder
Submerged Arc Hand Welder
Welder Helper

Oxyacetylene Welder
Oxyhydrogen Welder
Plasma Arc Welder
Production Line Welder
Electron-Beam Machine Welder Setter
Resistance Machine Welder Setter
Shielded-Metal Arc Welder
Structural Repair Welder
Tack Welder
Tool-and-Die Welder
Welding-Machine Feeder
Arc Welding-Machine Operator
Electro-Gas Welding-Machine Operator
Electron Beam Welding-Machine Operator
Electroslag Welding-Machine Operator
Friction Welding-Machine Operator
Gas Welding-Machine Operator
Gas-Metal Arc Welding-Machine Operator
Gas-Tungsten Arc Welding-Machine Operator
Welding-Machine-Operator Helper
Submerged Arc Welding-Machine Operator
Thermit Welding-Machine Operator
Ultrasonic Welding-Machine Operator
Welding-Machine Tender
Welding Tester
Weld Inspector

WORK PERFORMED

Welders work in a number of major industries. They help assemble some of the largest and most important structures in the civilized world.

Building Construction

Many welders work in the building construction industry. This is especially common in erecting large buildings of steel and concrete. For a multistory office building, for example, welders connect beams, steel reinforcing rods, and other parts of the steel superstructure. They perform similar work in building other structures such as sports stadiums, manufacturing facilities, instructional buildings at schools and colleges, and warehouses. For buildings made of all types of materials, metal beams and other elements of the basic support structure must be welded.

Because welding is such an important facet of the construction industry, job openings for welders can occur in all kinds of settings across the United States and Canada. This includes large cities, suburban areas, and small towns. Some jobs, such as assembling components for prefabricated buildings, involve staying in one location and working in a shop environment. Others require traveling from one construction site to the next.

Road and Bridge Construction

Another major area of employment for welders is road and bridge construction. Welders help build guard rails, steel reinforcing portions of concrete highways, and bridges—including large bridges for major highways or small bridges for less-traveled roads. In addition to building new bridges, such work often consists of repairing existing structures.

Automobile Industry

Thousands of welders are employed in the automobile industry. They play an important part in assembling the millions of cars and trucks produced every year. For example, a welder in this industry may specialize in operating an automated welding machine as a part of a car assembly line. Or a welder might work in the auto repair industry instead of manufacturing. Such work might involve welding damaged exhaust pipes, radiators, or auto body parts. In fact, many people first master welding skills to perform this kind of work and then expand their skills into other welding areas.

Shipbuilding

Still another major area in which welding plays a key role is shipbuilding. Although ships are produced in much smaller quantities than cars, that factor may be offset by the tremendous size of many ships. Building just one ship can keep a large crew of workers busy for many months.

The work involved in shipbuilding can be quite rewarding. The end product may be an aircraft carrier, submarine, cargo ship, or supertanker. Helping construct such a huge structure can be an exciting process. And since such large amounts of metal must be used in building a single ship, the role played by welders is extremely important.

Aircraft Construction

Welders perform equally vital work in aircraft construction. They help construct huge jets and other commercial aircraft, small airplanes, helicopters, and a variety of military aircraft. Welders in this industry must meet special standards of performance due to safety regulations. They must work with great care and produce results that are free of errors. As with construction of ships, workers can experience special feelings of satisfaction when they see the end result of their efforts. For many people, the sense of accomplishment in building sophisticated flying machines can be substantial.

JOB TASKS

In these and other industries, the specific job tasks performed by welders include a variety of functions. Typical work completed by men and women in such roles might include the following:

- operating a welding machine in an auto assembly plant
- welding pipes in a new shopping mall
- repairing broken pipes in a manufacturing plant
- assembling the fuselage of a jumbo jet
- welding a boiler on a new cruise ship
- connecting steel bars that will reinforce the concrete structure of a bridge
- welding components of a multistory distillation system at an oil refinery
- joining together sections of equipment in a factory that makes farm equipment
- performing nontechnical functions such as buying welding supplies, attending safety classes, or filling out production reports

SKILLS AND APTITUDES NEEDED

Anyone interested in a welding career should have certain basic aptitudes and the ability to master additional skills. For most workers, these qualities will include most or all of the following:

1. good manual skills (ability to use tools, adequate hand-to-eye coordination)
2. attention to detail

3. patience
4. dependability
5. pride in doing a good job
6. awareness of safety considerations
7. dexterity
8. physical stamina
9. good eyesight (or eyesight that can be corrected with contact lenses or glasses)
10. a steady hand
11. curiosity and a willingness to learn

Of course individual traits vary, and you can compensate for some weaknesses with hard work or creative approaches. For instance, if you are not particularly dexterous, that ability can be improved with exercises or repetition of basic tasks. If you have not had enough experience with hand tools to know whether you can use them effectively, taking a shop class or experimenting on your own can give some indications of your potential. The main point is to be realistic about your abilities and aptitudes, and then compare them with the requirements of a welding career.

DEVELOPING WELDING SKILLS

You probably will need to complete some type of training program to become a welder. Most people acquire welding capabilities through one or more of these training options:

- industry-sponsored training programs
- government-sponsored training programs
- apprenticeships
- high school vocational programs
- trade and technical schools
- community and junior colleges
- technical colleges
- military training programs

A description of these alternatives is provided in Chapter 8. Whichever option you choose, it is important to realize that a short-term investment of your time can pay off for many years to come. Most welding programs take only weeks or months to complete, meaning that even if you do not enjoy going to school, the commitment on your part will be manageable. Anyone with motivation and the qualities described in the previous section should be able to complete one of these training programs successfully.

CHAPTER 7

JEWELRY MAKING

When you think of metalworking, the first image that comes to mind will probably be of a bridge, building, appliance, or some other relatively large structure. But the range of metalworking careers includes not just industrial applications, but also fine, detailed work. One career area of this type is working as a jeweler or jewelry repairer.

Jewelers and related workers make or repair various kinds of jewelry including necklaces, bracelets, rings, earrings, pins, and other forms of adornment. In the process, they may complete work that is quite detailed and very precise.

WORK PERFORMED

Typical work performed by a jeweler might include the following:

- setting precious and semiprecious stones in engagement rings and other types of rings while working in a small manufacturing plant

- repairing broken jewelry in a repair shop, where an ordinary day's work might include fixing broken clasps of necklaces and bracelets, adjusting the sizes of rings, or replacing jewels in rings or other items
- managing a small retail store where duties combine repairing jewelry, supervising employees, and managing the overall business operations
- making jewelry from designs produced by others, or designing new pieces and then assembling them

Following is a general job description for the positions of jeweler, jewelry jobber, and jewelry repairer, which appears in the *Dictionary of Occupational Titles*:

> Fabricates and repairs jewelry articles, such as rings, brooches, pendants, bracelets, and lockets: Forms model of article from wax or metal, using carving tools. Places wax model in casting ring, and pours plaster into ring to form mold. Inserts plaster mold in furnace to melt wax. Casts metal model from plaster mold. Forms mold of sand or rubber from metal model for casting jewelry. Pours molten metal into mold, or operates centrifugal casting machine to cast article...Cuts, saws, files, and polishes article, using handtools and polishing wheel. Solders pieces of jewelry together, using soldering torch or iron. Enlarges or reduces size of rings by sawing through band, adding or removing metal, and soldering ends together. Repairs broken clasps, pins, rings, and other jewelry by soldering or replacing broken parts. Reshapes and restyles old jewelry, following designs or instructions,

using handtools and machines, such as jeweler's lathe and drill. Smooths soldered joints and rough spots, using hand file and emery paper. May be designated according to metals fashioned as Goldsmith (jewelry-silver.); Platinumsmith (jewelry-silver.); Silversmith (jewelry-silver.)

The type of work setting varies widely. Persons employed in the manufacturing of jewelry may work in a large shop or factory, while those employed at the retail level may work in a large department store or a small jewelry store. In a retail setting, the job may include interacting with customers in addition to the hands-on work performed. In some situations, jewelers or jewelry repairers may operate their own small businesses.

JOB TITLES

The U.S. Department of Labor lists dozens of job titles for work in the jewelry industry. Some examples are as follows:

Annealer
Assembler
Bracelet and Brooch Maker
Bracelet Maker, Novelty
Caster
Caster Helper
Chain-Maker, Hand

Chain-Maker, Machine
Chain Mender
Die Cutter
Die Maker
Driller
Earring Maker
Engraving Supervisor
Goldsmith
Jewelry-Engraving Supervisor
Jigsawyer
Lathe Hand
Lathe Operator
Link Assembler
Linker
Locket Maker
Melter
Mesh Cutter
Molder, Bench
Platinumsmith
Ring Maker
Ring Stamper
Rolled-Gold Plater
Roller
Sample Maker
Scraper
Scratch Brusher
Silversmith
Solderer

Stringer-Up, Soldering Machine
Supervisor, Jewelry Department
Trophy Assembler
Watch-Band Assembler
Wire Drawer

SPECIAL JOB FEATURES

One of the most interesting aspects of the jewelry-making field is the potential for creativity. While in some cases the work may consist of duplicating designs in accordance with specific instructions provided by a supervisor, in others the jeweler may develop his or her own designs. For example, a jeweler in a small shop may create a brooch or pendant without consulting a design or model, or may fashion a piece of jewelry based on the special request of a customer. This can add an element of artistic creativity that greatly enhances the enjoyment of job performance.

Another important feature of the work of jewelers is the need to be conscious of security. By its very nature, jewelry is often extremely valuable. Items made of precious metals such as gold or silver may be worth hundreds or thousands of dollars, and this value can be increased even more when gems such as diamonds, rubies, sapphires, or emeralds are added. As a result, working with jewelry can include significant financial responsibilities.

Jewelers and related workers must not only be honest themselves, but they must also guard against possible dishonesty by others. Their job duties may include the following:

- maintaining an accurate, up-to-date inventory of jewelry and working materials
- storing jewelry and components in locked storage areas and making certain they are secured when not being used
- operating electronic alarms and other advanced security systems
- treating working materials with great care to avoid damage or loss

CAREER ADVANTAGES

Each career area has its own particular advantages, but those of the jewelry-making field set it apart in some ways from some other metalworking careers. Some of these advantageous factors are as follows:

Comfortable working conditions. Unlike many other persons who work with metal, jewelers and related workers often work in comfortable, attractive, indoor settings. These may range from a shop environment to a retail store.

Limited physical requirements. Although good eyesight and the ability to work well with one's hands are necessary, there is no need for physical strength, climbing ability, or other such physically demanding job traits. Thus persons who may not feel suited to the rigors of a career as an ironworker, for instance, may find jewelry making a more appropriate metalworking field.

Potential links with other careers. Men and women who start out in this field may find that it leads to other career areas. For example, some jewelry-making jobs might lead to supervisory positions in retail stores, sales positions, or other related work.

TRAINING OPTIONS

Jewelers and related workers usually acquire their skills through on-the-job training or by attending a trade or technical school, or through a combination of these options. A high school diploma may be needed before pursuing one of these training approaches, but collegiate study is not necessary.

Students who attend trade or technical schools take classes covering such subjects as basic jewelry-making skills, repair techniques, use and care of tools and machines, casting, and polishing. They may also study math and blueprint reading. The length of programs varies from one school to the next, with some programs taking as few as six months to complete and others lasting two years or more.

Some manufacturers and other employers offer in-house training programs. Students learn skills similar to those in trade school programs, but usually with special emphasis on the specific needs of the employer. For example, a company that provides engraving services may spend a substantial amount of training time on this skill, while another company that does not specialize in engraving may skip the subject entirely. A firm that produces a limited number of jewelry types may deal only with those particular products in its training activities.

In any case, some type of training usually is necessary to work in this field. More information on training opportunities is provided in Chapter 8, and schools that offer training for jewelers are listed in Appendix B.

GETTING TRAINED

Working with metal requires special knowledge and skills. To pursue a career in this field, you will need to complete one or more of the following steps:

1. *Learn informally on the job.* Some employers will hire inexperienced workers and then expect them to learn metalworking skills by observing other workers or having more experienced personnel teach them the basics. This is more common with nonunion employers and small companies than with large corporations. Such measures are in some ways less desirable than structured training programs since they do not cover as much detail. Also, informal training options are not always available, especially in some of the more complex metalworking fields.

2. *Participate in a formal on-the-job training program.* This might consist of an apprenticeship sponsored by a company, a trade union, or both. Or it might be a short-term program offered by an employer. In either

case, each participant will follow a structured approach, and completion of such a program normally will be required of all new employees.

3. *Go to school.* For some metalworking fields, the best way to get started is to attend a school offering training in the appropriate area. This might be a vocational school, a trade or business school, or a two-year college. Which one depends upon the nature of the program and several other factors that will be discussed later in this chapter.

Whichever training approach you take, careful advance planning will help you avoid problems along the way. Be sure to ask yourself questions such as the following:

- What training options exist in the field in which I am interested?
- Are training programs in metalworking available in my geographical area?
- If training programs are not located nearby, am I willing to travel the necessary distance to participate in one?
- Am I willing to go on to more school after high school if need be?
- If I have a choice between attending a school or college and participating in on-the-job training, which choice will be best for me?
- Will I have to pay for training? If so, where will I obtain the funds?

In finding the answers to questions such as these, you will be taking the initial steps in preparing for a metalworking career.

APPRENTICESHIPS

In some metalworking fields, an effective way to learn the trade is to serve as an apprentice. This special learning format involves working under the supervision of one or more persons who have already had substantial job experience and are therefore qualified to help pass their knowledge on to newcomers.

Serving an apprenticeship is one of the oldest ways of learning a trade or craft. Since medieval times, workers have used this method of learning skilled trades. At one time, this was about the only way to master many trades, with basic techniques kept secret by practitioners and shared only with other workers in the field and apprentices.

In modern times, apprenticeships still play an important role in some areas, even though they are not as dominant as they once were. For persons who want to become sheet-metal workers, for instance, an apprenticeship is the preferred approach.

Apprenticeship in Sheet-Metal Working

The Sheet Metal Workers International Association, a major union, requires its members to complete a structured apprenticeship. This training is cosponsored by an organization of contractors, the Sheet Metal and Air Conditioning Contractors' National Association, through a fund established by both groups and called the National Training Fund. Persons who undergo such training must complete approximately eight thousand hours of supervised job experience and nearly six hundred hours of instruction over a period of about four years. As described in a publication of the National Training Fund, "Careers in Sheet Metal," apprentices cover the following as they progress through the four-year period:

First Year
- Sign written agreements setting out program terms
- Begin working on the job
- Begin attending classes (which may meet one or more evenings per week, or may be held during the day)
- Complete the probationary period (if required)
- Learn basics of pattern layout and development
- Learn basics of drafting
- Practice use of hand tools
- Learn how to apply mathematics to the sheet-metal trade
- Master safety concepts and procedures

Second Year
- Continue working on the job
- Continue classroom training

- Emphasize increased knowledge of metals and their substitutes
- Develop skills in basic plan and specification reading
- Strengthen knowledge of triangulation, radial line and parallel line development

Third Year
- Begin to work with less supervision from experienced workers
- Continue on-the-job training
- Continue classroom instruction
- Learn about solar installation
- Master soldering techniques
- Study hoisting and rigging
- Learn about energy management and retrofitting of environmental systems

Fourth Year
- Work with increasingly less supervision
- Read complex plans and specifications
- Increase knowledge of cooling, heating, and ventilation systems
- Master various welding techniques
- Understand functions of refrigeration components such as condensers and compressors

At the end of the four-year period, the man or woman who successfully completes this training earns the title of *journeyman.* This means that the individual becomes a full-fledged worker in the field with equal status of other experienced workers. Employers and coworkers can count on the person's ability to complete a variety of tasks competently and efficiently.

Machining Apprenticeships

Similar options are offered in machining and other metalworking trades. For example, the International Association of Machinists and Aerospace Workers operates a basic apprenticeship program in cooperation with employers. In its *Apprenticeship Training Manual,* the association notes the following responsibilities of apprentices:

1. To diligently and faithfully perform the work of the trade and to perform such other pertinent duties as may be assigned by the employer's supervisor of apprentices which are related to the apprentice's total training program.

2. To respect the property of the employer and abide by the rules and regulations of the employer, the union, and the committee.

3. To regularly attend and satisfactorily complete the required hours of related instruction as required under this apprenticeship program.

4. To maintain such records of work experience and training received on the job and in related instruction as may be required by the committee.

5. To develop safe working habits and conduct themselves in their work in such a manner as to assure their own safety and that of their fellow workers.

6. To work for the employer to whom indentured by the completion of apprenticeship unless terminated by the committee. Not to seek employment with another employer within the jurisdictional area of this program without prior clearance of the committee, the union, and the employer to whom indentured.

7. To conduct themselves, at all times, in a creditable, ethical, and moral manner, trying to realize that much time, money, and effort will be spent in affording the apprentice an opportunity to become a skilled journeyman.

Advantages of Apprenticeships

The apprentice approach to training offers a number of advantages. It is not hurried or condensed, providing plenty of time to master the work involved. Participants benefit from direct, on-the-job experience and frequent contact with experienced workers. At the same time, they are earning a regular income that increases as they gain experience and knowledge.

ON-THE-JOB TRAINING

Employers who do not rely on the apprenticeship system may offer their own training for new employees. In larger companies, such training may consist of a formal class for a group of new workers. In other situations, one-on-one instruction may be provided. For example, a man who runs a small machine shop may hire an inexperienced person and then teach basic skills as the two work together in an informal learning format not greatly different from an apprenticeship.

How do you find out about company-sponsored training? Sometimes, newspaper ads or other announcements about job openings will indicate that new workers are needed and that training will be provided to successful applicants. In other cases, you may need to contact the personnel office at a company that employs workers in metalworking fields and ask if special training is offered.

In a small shop setting, it may be worthwhile to talk to the owner and ask what possibilities may exist for on-the-job training. For instance, a person who operates a small aluminum siding firm may be willing to teach the basics of the business to an inexperienced newcomer.

GOVERNMENT-SPONSORED TRAINING PROGRAMS

Another training alternative is provided by special training programs supported through funding from government agencies. Sometimes these programs are sponsored by employers, sometimes by schools or colleges, and sometimes by combinations of the two or by other agencies.

A prime example is training made possible through the Job Training Partnership Act (JTPA). This is a special initiative of the U.S. government to reduce unemployment and provide trained workers in a variety of fields. Under this program, organizations such as companies or schools apply for grants to provide job-specific training. Those who are funded then enroll participants who complete the training that qualifies them to land good jobs. For example, an employer who needs more welders or machine operators may receive JTPA funds to train and place fifteen workers over a six-month period. After this time period, the program is no longer offered unless another grant is obtained. The short-term nature of each program means that students are not tied up over a long period of time and that training is directly related to the need for new workers by a single company or within a given geographical area.

To qualify for such training, you must meet certain eligibility requirements based on family income, previous employment status, age, or other factors. To find out more, check with the local JTPA Private Industry Council (PIC) or the nearest branch of your state employment office.

PROGRAMS OFFERED BY SCHOOLS
AND COLLEGES

In some metalworking fields, one of the best options available is to enroll in a trade school or two-year college that offers the appropriate training. For instance, classes in machining and welding are offered by many such institutions at both the trade school and collegiate levels. Programs for jewelers are offered by a number of schools, though not usually at the college level. On the other hand, sheet-metal work and ironwork usually are learned through industry-sponsored training rather than schools.

Choosing the Right Type of School for You

If you are interested in a subject that is taught in trade or technical schools, it is important to take your time in selecting the school that will be best for you. This may sound simple, but you can make a major mistake by enrolling in a program without checking it out or considering similar programs offered by other schools. Each school has its own strengths and weaknesses, ranging from the quality of its instructional equipment to the kind of reputation it has with employers.

In taking a look at any school, it's important to realize exactly what kind of institution it is and how this compares with others. Is it a trade or technical school? A technical college? A junior or community college? The terms may sound similar, but there can be important differences.

Trade school. For example, a local school may offer a machine shop program in which you are potentially interested. If it is a trade school, one of the advantages will be that the program can be completed in a relatively short time. Only technical or business courses will be offered, and you proabably will not have to take classes outside your field of study such as English, history, or other nontechnical subjects. Upon completing the required courses, you will earn a diploma or certificate rather than a degree.

Two-year college. The approach will be somewhat different at a two-year college. The term *two-year* can be somewhat misleading, for some programs can be completed in substantially less time. The term really refers to the highest level offered by a school, which in the case of two-year colleges is the associate degree.

Names of colleges of this type also can be confusing. Community colleges, junior colleges, and technical colleges can be identical in some cases but different in others. For example, in some states, technical colleges are exactly the same as community colleges. In other states, technical colleges differ in that they do not offer courses that can be transferred to four-year schools. At any rate, these differences among two-year colleges are usually insignificant for persons interested in metalworking fields. However, it may be important to establish that a school's name is truly accurate. Some trade schools refer to themselves as colleges but do not actually offer college-level work. Some others are called institutes, and in this case the school might qualify as a college or instead might actually be a trade school, depending on the type of programs offered.

What is significant is that in two-year colleges, you can pursue a more comprehensive selection of courses than in a trade school, with the end result being a college degree. To earn an associate degree, you will need to complete not only the required courses in metalworking, but also some other general courses such as English composition, sociology, psychology, or history. These courses usually are transferrable to four-year schools, which may not seem to matter now but may prove helpful if you ever want to pursue additional studies in the future. They also help you become a more well-rounded person and potentially a better employee.

If you are not interested in an associate degree, most two-year colleges also offer shorter programs leading to diplomas or certificates. These programs are much like those offered by trade schools, with few nontechnical courses required and no promise that credits will transfer to four-year schools.

Whether offered at the associate level or not, most two-year college programs offer the advantage of low costs. In some cases, expenses reach only a fraction of those charged by private trade schools. They may also provide a high level of respectability due to the status sometimes associated with college-level work.

Checking Out a School

To check out the features of any given school, take the following steps:

1. Obtain a copy of the school's catalog and study it closely. Check out whether it offers any programs in metalworking fields such as machining or welding and, if so, whether students earn diplomas, certificates, or associate degrees. You can often do this online by visiting a college's web site.

2. Read through the catalog and review any information about accreditation, special programs, financial aid, and other details.

3. Take a careful look at the catalog descriptions of programs in which you are interested. Review such details as how long it might take to complete a program and what kinds of courses are required.

4. Study any other information you can find in the catalog or through other sources. For example, don't overlook the course-by-course descriptions provided in most catalogs, often in the back of the publication. These summaries can let you know a great deal about the content of any program. Similarly, information on the success of graduates in obtaining jobs can prove

helpful. Does the school have a career planning office? If so, that is a good sign in itself, and this office should be able to provide figures on the track record of previous students in finding jobs in their fields.

5. Visit the school if possible. For local schools this should not be a problem, but if you are considering going away to school, be wary of selecting a school on the basis of its publications. Every school tries to present itself in the best possible light, but you could be disappointed without a firsthand look in advance. In the process, pay attention to such factors as the condition of shops or labs and the availability of modern equipment.

6. Look carefully at costs. When comparing one school to the next, be sure to find out just what costs are involved. Some schools are relatively inexpensive, while others cost thousands of dollars in annual tuition and fees.

In general, schools that do not receive local or state government funding are the most costly. These include private two-year colleges, which are nonprofit, and private trade and technical schools, also known as proprietary schools, which are operated as businesses, with their main purpose to make a profit for their owners. As a result, they tend to charge significantly more than public institutions. To some extent, the extra costs can be offset by providing students with grants, scholarships, or loans. Be careful about taking loans, however—they can result in a large debt that must be paid back over a period of months or years following completion of studies.

Expenses are usually much lower at public, two-year colleges. Most of these schools follow an admissions policy in which anyone can attend who might benefit from an instructional program. To keep access open, they keep tuition and other costs as low as possible—usually less than $1,500 per year—and financial aid is provided for students who need assistance. From a dollar-and-cents viewpoint, the deal is hard to beat.

In addition to the cost of your course work, you will need to compare living expenses if you plan to attend school away from home. Examine the costs of rent, utilities, transportation, and food in the community where the school is located. In some cases, you may decide that although the school's rates are reasonable, the cost of living in the area is too high. Particularly for short-term programs, it is easier to attend a school close to home.

7. Make sure the school is accredited. Most schools are licensed by the state in which they are located, but this really means little more than that they have purchased a business license or registered with the state government. If possible, attend only a school or college that is fully accredited. A trade school, for instance, might be accredited by the Accrediting Commission of

Career Schools and Colleges of Technology. A two-year college should be accredited by a regional association such as the North Central Association of Colleges and Schools.

PAYING FOR TRAINING

One of the advantages of an apprenticeship or other on-the-job training is that you do not have to pay for it. Instead, you normally receive pay while the training is conducted. Even though the rate of pay probably will be lower than that of fully trained workers, this can be a significant advantage.

Attending a trade school or two-year college is another matter. Most schools charge tuition, fees, and other costs, which can add up to a substantial total. Such costs may include the following:

- *Tuition.* This may be hundreds or even thousands of dollars, depending on the school.
- *Application fees.* These may be required before enrollment; amounts vary.
- *Books.* Costs vary; many books may be $50 to $100 each.
- *Supplies.* These may include welding rods, tools, or other necessary items.
- *Other fees.* These may include lab fees, activity fees, parking fees, and so forth.

GETTING FINANCIAL AID

Yes, trade schools and colleges may be expensive. But fortunately, a great deal of financial aid is available for students who need such assistance. This includes programs offered by the government, the schools themselves, and private sources.

Applying for Financial Aid

The key to obtaining financial assistance is to fill out the necessary application forms. Too often, students put this off until the last minute and then face delays in obtaining funds. If you need financial assistance, consult the financial aid office in a school in which you are interested and obtain the right forms. Then complete and submit them as soon as possible.

Some of the best programs available are sponsored by the U.S. government. To qualify for some of them, you must provide details about such matters as family income, assets, and debts. Although this may seem to require a lot of time and effort, the process may result in financial aid awards of hundreds or thousands of dollars—so don't be reluctant to take these steps! You probably will complete the U.S. Department of Education's Free Application for Federal Student Aid (FAFSA) plus some other forms unique to your state.

Check with a counselor to obtain forms. The forms can be obtained directly from the U.S. Department of Education, from high school guidance counselors, and from financial aid offices in colleges and trade schools.

Typical Aid Programs

Millions of students receive financial aid each year from the federal government as well as other sources to pursue postsecondary education. Some of these programs include:

Pell Grants. These are outright grants for students. They are not loans and never have to be repaid. Eligibility is based on need, so the more help you need, the more dollars are made available.

Supplemental Educational Opportunity Grants (SEOG). Like Pell Grants, these awards do not have to be repaid. A difference is that while everyone who qualifies for a Pell Grant receives one, the number of SEOG awards available at each school is limited. As a result, it is especially important to apply early for this program.

Special loan programs. A number of programs provide loans to attend school, with interest rates that are lower than conventional loans due to government backing. These include Perkins Loans (previously called National Direct Student Loans), Stafford Loans (formerly known as Guaranteed Student Loans or GSLs), and PLUS loans. Some of these loans are made to parents and others directly to students. An advantage is that you can take a long time to repay them if desired.

Work-study programs. Students in such programs earn wages by working in part-time jobs at a college or other area businesses authorized by the school.

In addition to these sources, you may be eligible for other assistance sponsored by the school you plan to attend, by professional organizations, or by other groups. Check with counselors or financial aid personnel for details about such programs.

CHAPTER 9

EARNINGS, BENEFITS, AND SPECIAL OPPORTUNITIES

EARNINGS

Persons employed in metalworking jobs tend to earn excellent wages and benefits. Earnings vary according to a number of factors, but the following examples may illustrate the earning potential of these fields:

- Union workers in the sheet-metal industry averaged more than $31 per hour in total compensation in 1997, according to the U.S. Department of Labor, and that figure has risen in recent years.
- The median weekly wage for tool and die makers is more than $700, according to the Department of Labor.
- According to the American Welding Society, starting wages for welders average anywhere from three to five times the minimum wage as established by the federal government. This translates to an average starting wage

of about $32,000 to $50,000 per year. In some situations, wages can go as high as ten times the minimum wage.

- Machinists and related workers earn wages that compare favorably with other metalworking careers. Their median 1996 weekly income was $440, and some earned more than $600 a week, according to the U.S. Department of Labor.
- Jewelers and those with similar jobs average more than $30,000 annually.

It is important to realize that wages can vary a great deal depending on how long a person has worked in the field, whether the worker is a member of a trade union, and other considerations. Other factors influencing wages can include the following:

Unionization. Companies that are "union shops" often pay higher wages than those where employees are not members of a union. In such cases, salaries and benefits are established in written agreements between the union and the employer, and they may be greater due to the union's bargaining power.

Location. Workers in urban areas tend to make more than those in rural areas, and Canadian wages may be higher when compared to U.S. figures due to differences in the value of currency.

Cost of living at the local level. Wages can be influenced greatly by the local cost of living. In Alaska, for instance, a gallon of milk or a house payment may cost more than twice the amount for an equivalent item in South Dakota or Arkansas. Wages must therefore be higher to compensate for these differences.

National economic conditions. The state of the national economy in Canada or the United States plays an important part in determining wages and salaries. In hard times, wages tend to increase slowly. During times of inflation wages go up more rapidly—however, so do living expenses, so don't be misled.

Skills required in different jobs. Very complex metalworking jobs often pay higher wages than those requiring more basic skills. For example, workers who are trained to use computerized equipment will probably earn more than helpers who perform general duties. Also, persons in apprenticeship roles earn less than those who have moved past this status.

Competition. The level of competition with other firms employing metalworking personnel can have an impact on wages. This is especially true for nonunion settings. If a local company increases wages, other companies in the same area may need to do the same to keep from losing workers. On the other hand, if there is little local competition, an employer may be able to get away with paying lower wages.

Company business conditions. A shipbuilding company that has just won a large government contract may be able to offer high pay. A manufacturing firm that is losing money may need to reduce wages. How well a given company is doing can affect its ability to pay top wages. Similarly, a new company may have to establish itself more firmly before it is able to pay high salaries.

BENEFITS

Hourly wages or monthly salaries are only part of the story. Along with basic wages, most employers offer a variety of fringe benefits to their employees. Benefits are extremely important considerations and should be examined carefully in any employment situation.

Fringe benefits can vary substantially. Factors affecting how they are determined include whether employees are unionized, whether a worker has full-time or part-time status, and patterns the employer has followed in the past.

Persons holding jobs in metalworking fields may receive benefits such as these:

- retirement or pension funds
- medical insurance
- paid vacation time
- paid sick leave
- workers' compensation in case of injury
- Social Security benefits
- dental insurance

- optical insurance
- profit-sharing plans

In considering any job, fringe benefits should be looked at carefully along with wages themselves. An advantage of working for a large company or being a union member is that fringe benefits may be more attractive than with small companies or some nonunion employers.

JOB OPENINGS

Thousands of jobs become available in the metalworking industry every year. Some of these positions are needed to replace persons who retire, die, or leave the field for other jobs. Others represent new positions created as industries expand or new businesses open. The U.S. Department of Labor estimates the following numbers of persons are employed in selected metalworking fields:

Sheet-metal working 110,000

Machining and tool programming. 393,000

Machine operation. 1,512,000
(includes those who work with plastic)

Welding 453,000

Jewelry making 32,000

Job openings will fluctuate from year to year according to economic conditions, but the long-term prospects for job openings look good in these fields for persons with the right training and abilities.

EXPANDING OPPORTUNITIES FOR WOMEN AND MINORITIES

Most metalworking fields have been dominated by white men due to a variety of social and historical factors. However, in recent years, more and more workers from traditionally underrepresented groups have entered these fields.

Female workers, for example, now hold many jobs in metalworking. Large numbers of women first entered the workforce in the 1940s during World War II, when American and Canadian factories hired women to take the place of men who were serving in the military. Female workers played a key role in the production of war equipment such as ships, airplanes, guns, and tanks, as well as automobiles and other domestic goods.

While many of these women left or were forced out of their jobs at the end of the war, the decades since then have seen a marked change in women's roles. Today, the idea of women workers in metalworking fields is no longer revolutionary. In fact, some employers go out of their way to hire female workers as they strive to diversify their workforce.

A similar practice is followed by many schools and colleges in recruiting students for training programs in technical fields such as metalworking. Not only do they welcome female students in such fields, but many also offer special financial aid and support programs for students. Examples include scholarship programs to promote gender equity or assist single parents and homemakers. Such programs may provide tuition, fees, and special counseling services. In some cases, even transportation and child care expenses may be provided.

Members of minority racial and ethnic groups also find more opportunities than ever in metalworking fields. Hiring more members of minority groups is a common policy in many corporations and other organizations. Also, numerous scholarships and academic support programs focus on minorities. Many schools and colleges offer special grants, scholarships, counseling services, or other support for minority students.

CAREER POSSIBILITIES FOR THE HANDICAPPED

Some metalworking jobs provide significant possibilities for men or women with handicaps or disabilities. Opportunities depend upon such factors as the type of disability and the extent to which it is restrictive. A person who cannot walk, for example, may not be able to function effectively as an ironworker. But the same individual may function quite well as a jeweler or as an operator of some types of metal-working machines.

Some employers and professional organizations offer special assistance to handicapped persons. A good example is the IAM Cares program, a broad initiative that is sponsored by the International Association of Machinists and Aerospace Workers. This special initiative offers a Projects with Industry program, which helps disabled persons find and keep jobs, along with a Transitional Services for Handicapped Youths program to help young people adjust to the change from a school setting to the workplace.

Government agencies also provide a variety of support services for the disabled ranging from training to assistance in job placement. For information on services available in your area, contact the nearest vocational rehabilitation center.

CHAPTER 10

WHERE TO GO FROM HERE

To pursue a career in metalworking, you can take any of several paths. To get yourself started in the right direction, consider such steps as these:

1. Find out exactly what training programs are available in your area.
2. Apply for admission to a program that seems best suited to your goals and needs.
3. Visit local companies where metalworkers are employed to get a feel for the work involved.
4. Talk with counselors or educators about your prospects for a career in metalworking.
5. Find a job where training is provided, or start the educational program of your choice.

FINDING A JOB

Finding a job in metalworking can be accomplished in a number of ways. In some cases, the job search may take place after you have completed a training program. In others, training will be provided after you are hired.

In any case, the first step is to identify job openings. To locate job openings, consult the following:

- the classified advertising sections of newspapers
- ads in magazines that cater to metalworking professionals or other industrial personnel
- personnel offices of companies where you would like to work
- local employment service or job service offices

When you have identified an opening, you will probably have to fill out a written job application. If this is required, be sure to take your time in filling it out, and answer each question completely and honestly. Be as neat as possible, and double-check spelling and grammar. You can prepare ahead of time a list of your previous employers, including their names, addresses, and phone numbers; starting and ending dates of your employment; and starting and ending wage rates. Such information typically is requested on the application, and carrying a prepared list will save you from wracking your brain when you receive the application form.

HANDLING JOB INTERVIEWS

The next step may be to go through a job interview. If you are asked to sit for an interview, take the following steps:

Plan ahead. Take some time to plan ahead before the actual interview. For example, try to anticipate possible questions and practice answering them.

Dress neatly. Don't make the mistake of showing up for an interview looking sloppy. Be sure to wear clean, neat clothes and present a good overall image.

Be on time. Always be on time for any interview. Being late can make an employer wonder if you will have problems reporting to work on time after you are hired.

Remain calm. This may be easier said than done, but try to stay as calm as possible. Don't worry about possible mistakes, but just be yourself. Keep in mind that if this job does not materialize, something even better may be awaiting you.

Sooner or later, you will find that initial job. And with hard work and a positive attitude, you can be well on the way to a rewarding career in metalworking!

FURTHER READING

Althouse, Andrew (editor). *Modern Welding.* Goodheart-Wilcox Company, 1997.

American Welding Society. "Welding and Joining."

Finch, Richard. *Welder's Handbook: A Complete Guide to Mig, Tig, Arc and Oxyacetylene Welding.* H.P. Books, 1997.

Garvey, Lonny D. *Opportunities in the Machine Trades.* NTC, 1994.

International Association of Machinists and Aerospace Workers. "Apprenticeship and Policy Manual."

National Training Fund. "Careers in Sheet Metal."

Remus, Tim. *The Ultimate Sheet Metal Fabrication Book.* Wolfgang Publications, 1999.

Sacks, Raymond J. *Essentials of Welding.* Bennett Publishing, 1984.

U.S. Department of Labor. *Dictionary of Occupational Titles.* 1992.

U.S. Department of Labor. *Occupational Outlook Handbook,* 1998–99.

TRADE AND TECHNICAL SCHOOLS OFFERING METALWORKING PROGRAMS

The following private trade and technical schools are among those offering instructional programs in at least one of the program areas covered in this book. Some schools offer only one program (for example, welding, machining, or jewelry design) while others offer several. For more details, call or visit schools close to your home, or write and request program information.

Also check out the RWM Vocational School database at www.rwm.org. Some listings here are provided courtesy of RWM.

Alaska

Testing Institute of Alaska
    2114 Railroad Avenue
    Anchorage, AK 99501

Hutchinson Career Center
 3750 Geist Road
 Fairbanks, AK 99709

Arizona

Center for Employment
 1198 South Fourth Avenue
 Yuma, AZ 85364

Navajo Community College
 Tsaile, AZ 86556

Schweiger's School of Basic Refrig., A/Cond., & Heating
 4518 Northwest Grand Avenue
 Glendale, AZ 85301

Arkansas

Central Arkansas Automotive and Trade School
 710 Broadway
 Little Rock, AR 72201

California

American River College
 4700 College Oak Drive
 Sacramento, CA 95841

CA Human Dev. Corp/Ctr. for Employment Training
 2895 Teepee
 Stockton, CA 95202

California Inst. of Jewelry Training
  4020 El Camino Avenue, Suite B1
  Sacramento, CA 95821

California Institute of Trades
  1910 West Palmyra Avenue, #62
  Orange, CA 95476

Cal-Trade Welding School
  7115 Bacchini Avenue
  Sacramento, CA 95828

Center for Employment Training
  701 Vine Street
  San Jose, CA 95110

Central Valley Opportunity Center Inc.
  1994 Rockerfeller
  Ceres, CA 95380

Consolidated Welding Schools
  4343 East Imperial Highway
  Lynwood, CA 90262

Delancey Street Academy
  600 Embarcadero
  San Francisco, CA 94115

Edutek Professional College
  5952 El Cajon Boulevard
  San Diego, CA 92115

Gemological Institute of America
  5345 Armada Drive
  Carlsbad, CA 92008

Golden State College
  1690 Universe Circle
  Oxnard, CA 93033

SUTECH School of Vocational and Technical Training
  3427 East Olympic Boulevard
  Los Angeles, CA 90023

Connecticut

Baran Institute of Technology
  15 Kimberly Avenue
  West Haven, CT 06525

Florida

First Inst. of Gemology & Jewelry Schl. of Florida
  220 Miracle Mile
  Coral Gables, FL 33134

Florida Jewelry & Watch Academy
  115 East Palmetto Park Road
  Boca Raton, FL 33432

Miami Jewelry Inst.
  561 Northwest Thirty-second Street
  Miami, FL 33127

Modern Schools
  100 Northwest Thirty-seventh Avenue
  Miami, FL 33125

Stewart's Intl. School for Jewelers
  651 West Indiantown Road
  Jupiter, FL 33458

Illinois

BIR Training Center
  3601 West Devon Avenue, Suite 205
  Chicago, IL 60659

Illinois Welding School
  5901 Washington Street
  Bartonville, IL 61607

The Quincy Technical School
  501 North Third Street
  Quincy, IL 62301

Indiana

ITT Technical Institute
  4919 Coldwater Road
  Fort Wayne, IN 46825

Louisiana

Bayou Technical Institute
  7818 Earhart Boulevard
  New Orleans, LA 70125

M. Weeks Welding Lab. Testing
  2707½ East Napoleon
  Sulphur, LA 70663

Nick Randazzo Voc. Train. Inst.
  1415 Whitney Avenue
  Gretna, LA 70053

Maryland

Cumberland Valley Technology Center
  319 West Howard Street
  Hagerstown, MD 21740

Delta School of Trades
  5418 Pulaski Highway
  Baltimore, MD 21205

Massachusetts

Boston Technical Center Inc.
  BMIP, 22 Drydock Avenue
  Boston, MA 02210

North Bennet Street School
  39 North Bennet
  Boston, MA 02113

Minnesota

Dunwoody Institute
  818 Wayzata Boulevard
  Minneapolis, MN 55403

Missouri

Ranken Technical Institute
  4431 Finney Avenue
  St. Louis, MO 63113

Sullivan Educational Centers
  1001 Harrison
  Kansas City, MO 64106

Vatterott College
  3925 Industrial Drive
  St. Ann, MO 63074

Vatterott Educational Center
  3854 Washington Avenue
  St. Louis, MO 63108

New Jersey

General Technical Institute
  1118 Baltimore Avenue
  Linden, NJ 07036

New York

Apex Technical School
  635 Avenue of the Americas
  New York, NY 10011

Joseph Bulova School
  40-24 62nd Street
  Woodside, NY 11377

Modern Welding School
  1842 State Street
  Schenectady, NY 12306

Ohio

Akron Machining Institute
  2959 Barber Road
  Barberton, OH 44203

Hobart School of Welding Technology
  400 Trade Square East
  Troy, OH 45373

Total Technical Institute
  6500 Pearl Road
  Panama Heights, OH 44130

Oklahoma

AAA Welding School
  9363 East Forty-sixth Street South
  Tulsa, OK 74145

Tulsa Welding School
  2545 East Eleventh Street
  Tulsa, OK 74104

Vatterott College
  3737 North Portland
  Oklahoma City, OK 73112

Pennsylvania

Commonwealth Technical Institute
  727 Goucher Street
  Johnstown, PA 15905

Dean Institute of Technology
  1501 West Liberty Avenue
  Pittsburgh, PA 15226

Fayette Inst. of Commerce & Technology
  45 West Kerr Street
  P.O. Box 136
  Uniontown, PA 15401

Johnson Technical Institute
  3427 North Main Avenue
  Scranton, PA 18508

New Castle School of Trades
  Route 422, Road 1
  Pulaski, PA 16143

O.S. Johnson Technical Institute
  3427 North Main Avenue
  Scranton, PA 18508

Penn Commercial, Inc.
  82 South Main Street
  Washington, PA 15301

Triangle Tech., Inc.
  P.O. Box 551
  Dubois, PA 15801

Welder Training & Testing Institute
  729 East Highland Street
  Allentown, PA 18103

Tennessee

William R. Moore School of Technology
  1200 Poplar Avenue
  Memphis, TN 38104

Texas

American Trade Institute
  6627 Maple Avenue
  Dallas, TX 75235

American Weld Testing
  921 Broadway
  Pasadena, TX 77506

ATI-Career Training Center
  2531 West North Highway
  Dallas, TX 75220

Capitol City Trade & Technical School
  205 East Riverside Drive
  Austin, TX 78704

Gulf Coast Trades Center
  FM 1375 West
  New Waverly, TX 77358

M. Weeks, Welding Laboratory Testing & School
  4405 Highway 347
  Nederland, TX 77627

San Antonio Trade School
  117 West Martin Street
  Del Rio, TX 78840

Texas Vocational School
  1913 South Flores
  San Antonio, TX 78204

Western Technical Institute
  1000 Texas Avenue
  El Paso, TX 79951

Washington

Perry Technical Institute
  2011 West Washington Avenue
  Yakima, WA 98903

COLLEGES OFFERING METALWORKING PROGRAMS

Many two-year colleges offer degree, diploma, or certificate programs to train machinists, welders, or other related workers.

These institutions may be called junior colleges, community colleges, or technical colleges. Most serve a local population, with relatively few having dormitories. This means the most convenient option is to attend a school of this type within driving distance of your home. It is possible to attend a two-year school in another city or state, but you will probably need to find an apartment or other housing on your own.

To learn what type of metalworking programs (if any) are offered by a given college, consult the school's catalog or contact its office of admissions.

Following is a list of some colleges that offer programs in metalworking fields. This is not intended to be a complete listing of all such schools, but rather a sampling of the institutions available. Address your correspondence to the admissions office of the school. For more details, contact a school near your home or in an area you find appealing.

Following the U.S. listing is a similar list of Canadian institutions.

U.S. COLLEGES

Alabama

Gadsden State Community College
  Gadsden, AL 35999

George C. Wallace State Community College
  Dothan, AL 36303

George Corley Wallace State Community College
  Selma, AL 36701

John C. Calhoun State Community College
  Decatur, AL 35602

Northwest Alabama Junior College
  Phil Campbell, AL 35581

Shelton State Community College
  Tuscaloosa, AL 35404

Alaska

Islands College
  Sitka, AK 99835

Ketchikan College
  Ketchikan, AK 99901

Arizona

Arizona Western College
  Yuma, AZ 85366

Central Arizona College
  Coolodge, AZ 85228

Cochise College
  Douglas, AZ 85607

Eastern Arizona College
  Thatcher, AZ 85552

Pima Community College
  Tucson, AZ 85709

Yavapai College
  Prescott, AZ 86301

Arkansas

Westark Community College
  Fort Smith, AR 72913

California

American River College
  Sacramento, CA 95841

Bakersfield College
  Bakersfield, CA 93305

Butte College
    Oroville, CA 95965

Cerritos Community College
    Norwalk, CA 90650

Chabot College
    Hayward, CA 94545

Citrus College
    Glendora, CA 91741

College of the Redwoods
    Eureka, CA 95501

Compton Community College
    Compton, CA 90221

De Anza College
    Cupertino, CA 95014

Fresno City College
    Fresno, CA 93741

Kings River Community College
    Reedley, CA 93654

Long Beach City College
    Long Beach, CA 90808

Los Angeles Harbor College
    Wilmington, CA 90744

Los Angeles Trade and Technical College
    Los Angeles, CA 90015

Modesto Junior College
  Modesto, CA 95350

Orange Coast College
  Costa Mesa, CA 92628

Rio Hondo College
  Whittier, CA 90601

San Diego City College
  San Diego, CA 92101

San Joaquin Delta College
  Stockton, CA 95207

Ventura College
  Ventura, CA 93003

Yuba College
  Marysville, CA 95901

Colorado

Arapahoe Community College
  Littleton, CO 80120

Community College of Denver
  Denver, CO 80217

Front Range Community College
  Westminster, CO 80030

Otero Junior College
  La Junta, CO 81050

Pikes Peak Community College
  Colorado Springs, CO 80906

Pueblo Community College
  Pueblo, CO 81004

Trinidad State Junior College
  Trinidad, CO 81082

Delaware

Delaware Technical and Community College
  Owen Campus
  Georgetown, DE 19947

Florida

Brevard Community College
  Cocoa, FL 32922

Central Florida Community College
  Ocala, FL 34478

Chipola Junior College
  Marianna, FL 32446

Daytona Beach Community College
  Daytona Beach, FL 32120

Indian River Community College
  Fort Pierce, FL 34981

Okaloosa-Walton Junior College
  Niceville, FL 32578

Pensacola Junior College
  Pensacola, FL 32504

Santa Fe Community College
  Gainesville, FL 32606

Seminole Community College
  Sanford, FL 32773

South Florida Community College
  Avon Park, FL 33825

Georgia

Bainbridge College
  Bainbridge, GA 31717

Coastal Georgia Community College
  Brunswick, GA 31520

Dalton College
  Dalton, GA 30720

Darton College
  Albany, GA 31707

Dekalb College
  Decatur, GA 30034

Hawaii

University of Hawaii-Honolulu Community College
  Honolulu, HI 96817

University of Hawaii-Kauai Community College
  Lihue, HI 96766

University of Hawaii-Maui Community College
  Kahului, HI 96732

Idaho

College of Southern Idaho
  Twin Falls, ID 83303

North Idaho College
  Coeur D'Alene, ID 83814

Ricks College
  Rexburg, ID 83460

Illinois

Belleville Area College
  Belleville, IL 62221

College of Du Page
  Glen Ellyn, IL 60137

Danville Area Community College
  Danville, IL 61832

Elgin Community College
  Elgin, IL 60123

Gem City College
  Quincy, IL 62301

Highland Community College
  Freeport, IL 61032

John A. Logan College
  Carterville, IL 62918

John Wood Community College
  Quincy, IL 62301

Joliet Junior College
  Joliet, IL 60431

Kankakee Community College
  Kankakee, IL 60901

Kishwaukee College
  Malta, IL 60150

Lewis and Clark Community College
  Godfrey, IL 62035

Lincoln Land Community College
  Springfield, IL 62794

McHenry County College
  Crystal Lake, IL 60012

Moraine Valley Community College
  Palos Hills, IL 60465

Oakton Community College
  Des Plaines, IL 60016

Rock Valley College
  Rockford, Il 61114

Triton College
  River Grove, IL 60171

Waubonsee Community College
  Sugar Grove, IL 60554

Indiana

Ivy Tech State College
Evansville, IN 47710

Ivy Tech State College
Fort Wayne, IN 46805

Ivy Tech State College
Indianapolis, IN 46206

Ivy Tech State College
Kokomo, IN 46903

Ivy Tech State College
Lafayette, IN 47903

Ivy Tech State College
Terre Haute, IN 47802

Vincennes University
Vincennes, IN 47591

Iowa

Des Moines Area Community College
Ankeny, IA 50021

Hawkeye Community College
Waterloo, IA 50704

Indian Hills Community College
Ottumwa, IA 52501

Iowa Central Community College
  Fort Dodge, IA 50501

Iowa Western Community College
  Council Bluffs, IA 51503

Kirkwood Community College
  Cedar Rapids, IA 52404

North Iowa Area Community College
  Mason City, IA 50401

Southeastern Community College
  West Burlington, IA 52655

Kansas

Allen County Community College
  Iola, KS 66749

Barton County Community College
  Great Bend, KS 67530

Butler County Community College
  El Dorado, KS 67042

Central College
  McPherson, KS 67460

Coffeyville Community College
  Coffeyville, KS 67337

Colby Community College
  Colby, KS 67701

Cowley County Community College
  Arkansas City, KS 67005

Dodge City Community College
  Dodge City, KS 67801

Fort Scott Community College
  Fort Scott, KS 66701

Garden City Community College
  Garden City, KS 67846

Haskell Indian Nations University
  Lawrence, KS 66046

Hutchinson Community College
  Hutchinson, KS 67501

Independence Community College
  Independence, KS 67301

Johnson County Community College
  Overland Park, KS 66210

Pratt Community College
  Pratt, KS 67124

Louisiana

Bossier Parish Community College
  Bossier City, LA 71111

Delgado Community College
  New Orleans, LA 70119

Maine

Northern Maine Technical College
  Presque Isle, ME 04769

Maryland

Catonsville Community College
  Baltimore, MD 21228

Cecil Community College
  North East, MD 21901

Chesapeake College
  Wye Mills, MD 21679

Garrett Community College
  McHenry, MD 21541

Michigan

Alpena Community College
  Alpena, MI 49707

Delta College
  University Center, MI 48710

Henry Ford Community College
  Dearborn, MI 48128

Kellogg Community College
  Battle Creek, MI 49017

Lake Michigan College
  Benton Harbor, MI 49022

Macomb County Community College
  Warren, MI 48093

Mid Michigan Community College
  Harrison, MI 48625

Monroe County Community College
  Monroe, MI 48161

Mott Community College
  Flint, MI 48503

Northwestern Michigan College
  Traverse City, MI 49686

Oakland Community College
  Bloomfield Hills, MI 48304

Schoolcraft College
  Livonia, MI 48152

West Shore Community College
  Scottville, MI 49454

Minnesota

Dakota County Technical College
  Rosemount, MN 55068

Hennepin Technical College
  Brooklynn Park, MN 55445

Ridgewater College
  Willmar, MN 56201

Rochester Community and Technical College
Rochester, MN 55904

University of Minnesota
Crookston, MN 56716

Mississippi

Coahoama Community College
Clarksdale, MS 38614

Copiah-Lincoln Community College
Wesson, MS 39191

East Central Community College
Decatur, MS 39327

Holmes Community College
Goodman, MS 39079

Itawamba Community College
Fulton, MS 38843

Meridian Community College
Meridian, MS 39307

Mississippi Delta Junior College
Moorhead, MS 38761

Mississippi Gulf Coast Community College
Perkinston, MS 39573

Northeast Mississippi Community College
Booneville, MS 38829

Northwest Mississippi Community College
  Senatobia, MS 38668

Pearl River Community College
  Poplarville, MS 39470

Southwest Mississippi Community College
  Summit, MS 39666

Missouri

Crowder College
  Neosho, MO 64850

East Central College
  Union, MO 63084

Jefferson College
  Hillsboro, MO 63050

Longview Community College
  Lee's Summit, MO 64081

Moberly Area Junior College
  Moberly, MO 65270

State Fair Community College
  Sedalia, MO 65301

Montana

Dawson Community College
  Glendive, MT 59330

Flathead Valley Community College
  Kalispell, MT 59901

Nebraska

Central Community College,
  Platte Campus
  Columbus, NE 68601

Mid-Plains Community College
  North Platte, NE 69101

Northeast Community College
  Norfolk, NE 68702

Western Nebraska Community College
  Scotts Bluff, NE 69361

Nevada

Community College of Southern Nevada
  Las Vegas, NV 89030

Truckee Meadows Community College
  Reno, NV 89512

Western Nevada Community College
  Carson City, NV 89703

New Hampshire

New Hampshire Community Technical College
  Berlin, NH 03570

New Hampshire Community Technical College
  Manchester, NH 03102

New Jersey

Middlesex County College
  Edison, NJ 08837

Passaic County Community College
  Paterson, NJ 07505

New Mexico

Eastern New Mexico University
  Clovis, NM 88101

Eastern New Mexico University
  Roswell, NM 88202

New Mexico Junior College
  Hobbs, NM 88240

Northern New Mexico Community College
  El Rito, NM 87530

New York

Dutchess Community College
  Poughkeepsie, NY 12601

Hudson Valley Community College
  Troy, NY 12180

Mohawk Valley Community College
  Utica, NY 13501

State University of New York
  College of Technology
  at Delhi
  Delhi, NY 13653

State University of New York
  College of Agriculture and Technology at Morrisville
  Morrisville, NY 13408

Suffolk County Community College
  Selden, NY 11784

Westchester Community College
  Valhalla, NY 10595

North Carolina

Anson Community College
  Polkton, NC 28135

Ashville Buncombe Technical College
  Ashville, NC 28801

Beaufort County Community College
  Washington, NC 27889

Caldwell Community College
  and Technical Institute
  Hudson, NC 28638

Catawba Valley Community College
  Hickory, NC 28602

Central Piedmont Community College
Charlotte, NC 28235

Coastal Carolina Community College
Jacksonville, NC 28546

College of the Albermarle
Elizabeth City, NC 27906

Forsyth Technical Community College
Winston-Salem, NC 27103

Isothermal Community College
Spindale, NC 28160

Mitchell Community College
Statesville, NC 28677

Pitt Community College
Greenville, NC 27835

Rockingham Community College
Wentworth, NC 27375

Southeastern Community College
Whiteville, NC 28472

Surry Community College
Dobson, NC 27017

Tri-County Community College
Murphy, NC 28906

Wake Technical Community College
Raleigh, NC 27603

Wilkes Community College
  Wilkesboro, NC 28697

North Dakota

Bismarck State College
  Bismarck, ND 58506

North Dakota State College of Science
  Wahpeton, ND 58076

Turtle Mountain Community College
  Belcourt, ND 58316

University of North Dakota
  Williston, ND 58802

Ohio

Belmont Technical College
  St. Clairsville, OH 43950

Columbus State Community College
  Columbus, OH 43215

Lakeland Community College
  Kirkland, OH 44094

Owens Community College
  Toledo, OH 43697

Sinclair Community College
  Dayton, OH 45402

Terra Community College
  Fremont, OH 43420

Washington State Community College
  Marietta, OH 45750

Oklahoma

Eastern Oklahoma State College
  Wilburton, OK 74578

Murray State College
  Tishomingon, OK 73460

Northeastern Oklahoma Agricultural
  and Mechanical College
  Miami, OK 74354

Northern Oklahoma College
  Tonkawa, OK 74653

Oklahoma City Community College
  Oklahoma City, OK 73159

Tulsa Community College
  Tulsa, OK 74135

Oregon

Blue Mountain Community College
  Pendleton, OR 97801

Central Oregon Community College
  Bend, OR 97701

Clackamas Community College
  Oregon City, OR 97045

Clatsop Community College
  Astoria, OR 97103

Lane Community College
  Eugene, OR 97405

Linn-Benton Community College
  Albany, OR 97321

Mount Hood Community College
  Gresham, OR 97030

Portland Community College
  Portland, OR 97280

Rogue Community College
  Grants Pass, OR 97527

Treasure Valley Community College
  Ontario, OR 97914

Umpqua Community College
  Roseburg, OR 97470

Pennsylvania

Community College of Allegheny County-Boyce
  Monroeville, PA 15146

Community College of Allegheny County-North
  Pittsburgh, PA 15237

Community College of Allegheny County-South
  West Mifflin, PA 15122

Community College of Beaver County
  Monaca, PA 15061

Westmoreland County Community College
  Youngwood, PA 15697

South Carolina

Aiken Technical College
  Aiken, SC 29802

Central Carolina Technical College
  Sumter, SC 29150

Chesterfield-Marlboro Technical College
  Cheraw, SC 29520

Denmark Technical College
  Denmark, SC 29042

Florence Darlington Technical College
  Florence, SC 29501

Greenville Technical College
  Greenville, SC 29606

Horry-Georgetown Technical College
  Conway, SC 29528

Orangeburg-Calhoun Technical College
  Orangeburg, SC 29118

Piedmont Technical College
  Greenwood, SC 29648

Spartanburg Technical College
  Spartanburg, SC 29305

Tri-County Technical College
  Pendleton, SC 29670

Trident Technical College
  Charleston, SC 29423

York Technical College
  Rock Hill, SC 29730

Tennessee

Chattanooga State Technical Community College
  Chattanooga, TN 37406

Cleveland State Community College
  Cleveland, TN 37320

Northeast State Technical Community College
  Blountville, TN 37617

State Technical Institute at Memphis
  Memphis, TN 38134

Texas

Angelina College
  Lufkin, TX 75902

Austin Community College
  Austin, TX 78752

Bee County College
  Beeville, TX 78102

Brazosport College
  Lake Jackson, TX 77566

Central Texas College
  Killeen, TX 76541

Cisco Junior College
  Cisco, TX 76437

Del Mar College
  Corpus Christi, TX 78404

El Paso Community College
  El Paso, TX 79998

Laredo Junior College
  Laredo, TX 78040

Lee College
  Baytown, TX 77522

Midland College
  Midland, TX 79705

Mountain View College
  Dallas, TX 75211

Navarro College
  Corsicana, TX 75110

Odessa College
  Odessa, TX 79764

Paris Junior College
  Paris, TX 75460

Ranger Junior College
  Ranger, TX 76470

South Plains College
  Levelland, TX 79336

Southwest Texas Junior College
  Uvalde, TX 78801

Tarrant County College
  Fort Worth, TX 76102

Wharton County Junior College
  Wharton, TX 77488

Utah

College of Eastern Utah
  Price, UT 84501

Dixie College
  Saint George, UT 84770

Salt Lake Community College
  Salt Lake City, UT 84130

Snow College
  Ephraim, UT 84627

Utah Valley State College
  Orem, UT 84058

Virginia

Central Virginia Community College
  Lynchburg, VA 24502

Dabney S. Lancaster Community College
  Clifton Forge, VA 24422

Danville Community College
  Danville, VA 24541

John Tyler Community College
  Chester, VA 23831

Mountain Empire Community College
  Big Stone Gap, VA 24219

New River Community College
  Dublin, VA 24084

Northern Virginia Community College
  Annandale, VA 22003

Patrick Henry Community College
  Martinsville, VA 24115

Southside Virginia Community College
  Alberta, VA 23821

Southwest Virginia Community College
  Richlands, VA 24641

Thomas Nelson Community College
  Hampton, VA 23670

Tidewater Community College
   Norfolk, VA 23510

Virginia Western Community College
   Roanoke, VA 24038

Wytheville Community College
   Wytheville, VA 24382

Washington

Big Bend Community College
   Moses Lake, WA 98837

Centralia College
   Centralia, WA 98531

Clark College
   Vancouver, WA 98663

Columbia Basin College
   Pasco, WA 99301

Grays Harbor College
   Aberdeen, WA 98520

Green River Community College
   Auburn, WA 98002

Highline Community College
   Des Moines, WA 98198

Olympic College
   Bremerton, WA 98337

Shoreline Community College
   Seattle, WA 98133

South Seattle Community College
    Seattle, WA 98106

Spokane Community College
    Spokane, WA 99207

Walla Walla Community College
    Walla Walla, WA 99362

West Virginia

Southern West Virginia
    Community and Technical College
    Logan, WV 25637

West Virginia University
    at Parkersburg
    Parkersburg, WV 26101

Wisconsin

Fox Valley Technical College
    Appleton, WI 54913

Lakeshore Technical College
    Cleveland, WI 53015

Madison Area Technical College
    Madison, WI 53704

Milwaukee Area Technical College
    Milwaukee, WI 53233

Waukesha County Technical College
    Pewaukee, WI 53072

Western Wisconsin Technical College
La Crosse, WI 54602

Wyoming

Casper College
Casper, WY 82601

Central Wyoming College
Riverton, WY 82501

Eastern Wyoming College
Torrington, WY 82240

Western Wyoming Community College
Rock Springs, WY 82902

CANADIAN COLLEGES

Alberta

Fairview College
11235-99 Avenue
P.O. Box 3000
Fairview, Alberta
T0H 1L0

Lakeland College
Vermillion Campus
Fort Kent Community Learning Centre
Box 150
Fort Kent, Alberta
T0A 1H0

Northen Alberta Institute of Technology (NAIT)
    11762-106th Street
    Edmonton, Alberta
    T5G 2R1

Southern Alberta Institute of Technology
    1301th-16 Avenue NW
    Calgary, Alberta
    T2M 0L4

British Columbia

British Columbia Institute of Technology (BCIT)
    3700 Willington Avenue
    Burnaby, British Columbia
    V5G 3H2

Camosun College
    Lansdowne Campus
    3100 Foul Bay Road
    3814 Carey Road
    Victoria, British Columbia
    V8Z 4C4

College of New Caledonia
    3330-22nd Avenue
    Prince George, British Columbia
    V2N 1P8

College of the Rockies
    2700 College Way
    P.O. Box 8500
    Cranbrook, British Columbia
    V1C 5L7

Kwantlen University College
  12666-72 Avenue
  P.O. Box 9030
  Surrey, British Columbia
  V3W 2M8

North Island College
  2300 Ryan Road
  Courtenay, British Columbia
  V9N 8N6

Northwest Community College
  5331 McConnell Avenue
  Terrace, British Columbia
  V8G 4X2

Selkirk College
  301 Frank Beinder Way
  P.O. Box 1200
  Castlegar, British Columbia
  V1N 3J1

University College of the Cariboo
  900 College Drive
  P.O. Box 3010
  Kamloops, British Columbia
  V2C 5N3

University College of the Fraser Valley
  33844 King Road
  RR #2
  Abbotsford, British Columbia
  V2S 7M9

Manitoba

Keewatin Community College
436 Seventh Street
P.O. Box 3000
The Pas, Manitoba
R9A 1M7

Red River College
2055 Notre Dame Avenue
Winnipeg, Manitoba
R3H 0J9

Winnipeg Technical Centre
P.O. Box 145
Winnipeg, Manitoba
R3Y 1G5

New Brunswick

Collège Communautaire du Nouveau Brunswick (CCNB)
Ministère de l'enseignement supérieur et du travail
C.P. 6000
500 Beverbrook Court
Frédéricton, New Brunswick
E3B 5H1

Newfoundland

College of the North Atlantic
P.O. Box 1693, 1 Prince Philip Drive
432 Massachusetts Drive
St-John's, Newfoundland

Northwest Territories

Aurora College
199 McDougal Road
P.O. Box 1290
Fort Smith, Northwest Territories
X0E 0P0

Nova Scotia

Nova Scotia Community College
P.O. Box 2212
5685 Leeds Street
Halifax, Nova Scotia
B3J 2X1

University College of Cape Breton
Place Bay Highway
P.O. Box 5300
Sydney, Nova Scotia
B1P 6L2

Ontario

Algonquin College of Applied Arts and Technology
Woodroffe Campus
1385 Woodroffe Avenue
Nepean, Ontario
K2G 1V8

Conestoga College of Applied Arts and Technology
Conestoga Campus
299 Doon Valley Drive
Kitchener, Ontario
N2G 4M4

Confederation College of Applied Arts and Technology
　　Thunder Bay Campus
　　1450 Nakina Drive
　　P.O. Box 398
　　Thunder Bay, Ontario
　　P7C 4W1

Fanshawe College of Applied Arts and Technology
　　London Campus
　　1460 Oxford Street East
　　P.O. Box 4005
　　London, Ontario
　　N5W 5H1

George Brown College of Applied Arts and Technology
　　500 MacPherson Avenue
　　P.O. Box 1015, Station B
　　Toronto, Ontario
　　M5T 2T9

Georgian College of Applied Arts and Technology
　　Barrie Campus
　　One Georgian Drive
　　Barrie, Ontario
　　L4M 3X9

Niagara College
　　300 Woodlawn Road
　　P.O. Box 1005
　　Welland, Ontario
　　L3B 5S2

Northen College of Applied Arts and Technology
  Porcupine Campus
  Highway 101 East
  P.O. Box 3211
  Timmins, Ontario
  P4N 8R6

Sault College of Applied Arts and Technology
  P.O. Box 60
  Sault Ste Marie, Ontario
  P6A 5L3

Seneca College of Applied Arts and Technology
  1750 Finch Avenue East
  Willowdale, Ontario
  M2J 2X5

St. Lawrence College
  2288 Parkedale Avenue
  Brockville, Ontario
  K6V 5X3

Prince Edward Island

Holland College
  140 Weymouth Street
  Charlottetown, Prince Edward Island
  C1A 4Z1

Saskatchewan

North West Regional College
  1381-101st Street
  Nth. Battleford, Saskatchewan
  S9A 0Z9

Parkland Regional College
  Box 790
  Melville, Saskatchewan
  S0A 2P0

Saskatchewan Institute of Applied Sciences and Technology
  400-119 Fourth Avenue South
  Saskatoon, Saskatchewan
  S7K 5X2

SELECTED ORGANIZATIONS RELATED TO METALWORKING

American Welding Society
55 Northwest Le Jeune Road
Miami, FL 33135

Associated General Contractors
of America, Inc.
1957 East Street NW
Washington, DC 20006

International Association of Machinists and Aerospace Workers
900 Machinists Place
Upper Marlboro, MD 20772

International Association of Machinists and Aerospace Workers
(Canada)
100 Metcalfe Street
Ottawa, Ontario
K1P 5M1

Jewelers of America
1185 Avenue of the Americas
New York, NY 10036

National Erectors Association
  1501 Lee Highway
  Arlington, VA 22209

National Tooling and Machining Association
  9300 Livingston Road
  Fort Washington, MD 20744

National Training Fund
  (Sheet Metal and Air Conditioning Industry)
  601 North Fairfax Street
  Alexandria, VA 22314

North American Die Casting Association
  9701 West Higgins Road
  Rosemont, IL 60018

Precision Machined Products Association
  6700 West Snowville Road
  Brecksville, OH 44141

Sheet Metal and Air Conditioning Contractors'
    National Association
  4201 Lafayette Center Drive
  Chantilly, VA 20151

Sheet Metal Workers' International Association
  1750 New York Avenue NW
  Washington, DC 20006

Tooling & Manufacturing Association
  1177 South Dee Road
  Park Ridge, IL 60008